S0-BIG-016

RS-232
Made Easy

MARTIN D. SEYER

American Bell, Inc.
a wholly-owned subsidiary of AT&T

RS-232

Made Easy

Connecting Computers, Printers, Terminals, and Modems

PRENTICE-HALL, INC.

Englewood Cliffs, NJ 07632

Library of Congress Cataloging in Publication Data

SEYER, MARTIN D.
  RS-232 made easy.

  Bibliography: p.
  Includes index.
    1. Computer interfaces—Standards—United States.
I. Title.
TK7887.5.S48 1984   001.64′404   83-13939
ISBN 0-13-783480-2 (case)
ISBN 0-13-783472-1 (pbk.)

Editorial/production supervision and
  interior design: Kathryn Gollin Marshak
Cover design: Lundgren Graphics
Manufacturing buyer: Gordon Osbourne

© 1984 by Prentice-Hall, Inc., Englewood Cliffs, New Jersey 07632

All rights reserved. No part of this book may be
reproduced, in any form or by any means,
without permission in writing from the publisher.

Printed in the United States of America

10 9 8 7 6 5 4 3 2

ISBN   0-13-783472-1 {P}
ISBN   0-13-783480-2 {C}

Prentice-Hall International, Inc., *London*
Prentice-Hall of Australia Pty. Limited, *Sydney*
Editora Prentice-Hall do Brasil, Ltda., *Rio de Janeiro*
Prentice-Hall Canada Inc., *Toronto*
Prentice-Hall of India Private Limited, *New Delhi*
Prentice-Hall of Japan, Inc., *Tokyo*
Prentice-Hall of Southeast Asia Pte. Ltd., *Singapore*
Whitehall Books Limited, *Wellington, New Zealand*

This book is dedicated to my wife, Melinda, and my children, Nathan and Taylor Macy, who supplied the patience, encouragement, and understanding necessary for me to write it.

Contents

Preface

Have you heard this before?

"Prior to dialing the phone number and connecting to services such as The Source,* ensure that the DTE is connected to the DCE with the RS-232-C cable provided for the serial ports. If you're using a standard terminal, all that is needed is an RS-232 interface and a modem or acoustic coupler. If you are accessing the system with a computer, merely add an asynchronous communication package and a modem. The speeds that are supported are 300 bps and 1200 bps over a full-duplex facility. The modem being used must support all RS-232-C-compatible signals for proper control of the transmission. The port on your device should be optioned for no parity, ASCII, with only one stop bit. The number you are dialing will be automatically answered. When you get the answer-back tone, go to "data." If you are using a printer with a serial interface, check to make sure that it is optioned for the correct speed, parity, character length, and polarity. If a null-modem cable is used between the terminal or computer and the printer, does it allow for either hardware or software flow control?"

What is all of this mumbo jumbo about options, communications, DTE, DCE, and RS-232-C? Is it something out of a Buck Rogers movie? Is E.T. trying to phone home? Is it a foreign language? No! It is terminology encountered by an increasing number of people involved with various aspects of personal and professional computing and communications. Whether you are providing on-line terminal

*The Source is a service mark of Source Telecomputing Corp.

access to a data base, connecting to a time-sharing system, or merely attaching a printer and a personal computer, these terms become extremely important. Where can you find out about connecting devices using serial interfaces, such as computers, printers, terminals, plotters, and modems? Look no further—you have come to the right place!

A standard for connecting business machines with serial interfaces has been in existence in the data processing and data communications industry for several years. The latest revision of this standard, known as RS-232-C, was established by the Electronic Industries Association of Washington, D.C., in 1969.

Interfaces adhering to this standard are incorporated into almost all mainframe computers, minicomputers, and associated peripherals. Also, as microcomputers, both business and personal, have become widespread, they too are supplying RS-232-C-type ports. With such increasing popularity, the need for a functional understanding of how to connect devices using RS-232 ports has never been greater.

Although widely used with computers, terminals, and printers, RS-232 is not very well understood. A single source providing functional insights into the definition and characteristic of the standard is needed. *RS-232 Made Easy* fills this void by providing both a framework for understanding serial communications and a thorough explanation of the functions of each lead of an RS-232 interface.

The international counterpart that resembles RS-232-C is known as CCITT V.24. CCITT stands for the International Telegraph and Telephone Consultative Committee. Both CCITT and EIA interfaces are similar. The basic difference is nomenclature. Throughout this book, references are made only to EIA RS-232-C (see Figure D-1), but the context is equally applicable to the V.24 standard. The reader need only remember that the naming conventions are different between the two.

Components of a communication environment can easily be likened to a railway system. Just as a train is transported along the rails between stations, so is information transferred between business machines. The elements of a railway system, such as the rails, trains, and stations (depots), provide an excellent illustration for comparison with the specifics of an RS-232 communication environment. Utilizing this analogy, both a general and detailed understanding can be achieved.

RS-232 Made Easy is organized in a manner that requires no prior knowledge of the subject. Its approach is from the standpoint of a first-time microcomputer buyer who is interested in, among other things, the game-playing capabilities of the computer. Of course, many machines are purchased by individuals, such as teachers, professors, hobbyists, business executives, engineers, analysts, programmers, and others, who have no intention of playing computer games. Nonetheless, a light hearted approach allows for a gradual movement into the seriousness of interfacing with RS-232. Chapters 1 and 2 establish the need for RS-232 and provide an understanding of prevalent communication terminology; thereafter, the explanation evolves into the specifics of RS-232-C. These specifics are first described in laymen's terms, using the railway system analogy. The technical definitions of the terms immediately follow the analogy and are indicated by the heading **RS-232.** Because data communication requirements dictate the various components of the standard, the analogy generally focuses on communication environments in which the RS-232-C interface is widely used. Communication terminology is denoted by the heading **DATA COMMUNICATIONS.** This same technique is applied in all chapters as the foundation is gradually expanded to provide the reader with a thorough understanding of serial interfaces.

The body of the book is followed by appendixes that serve as resources for users. They include excerpts from the RS-232-C standard and the relatively new RS-449 standard, which is intended gradually to replace RS-232-C. The tools that are useful when working in these serial environments are described. Also included is a listing of numerous available microcomputers, terminals, and printers and their corresponding RS-232-C pin assignments. *RS-232 Made Easy* proceeds to demonstrate, in a step-by-step manner, the interconnections of the printers, CRTs, and computers employing the RS-232-C interface. The cables for connecting such equipment are described. For example, if a user desires to connect an NEC Spinwriter* printer to an IBM PC† to allow printing of text created on some word processing package, the charts indicate which leads on the interface should be crossed. Factors relating to buffering and flow control can be easily addressed. Consulting the options checklist in Chapter 8 makes installation of the system easier and simplifies the selection of options in the areas of speed, parity, polarity, flow control, and echoplexing.

By providing a functional insight into RS-232 (and, correspondingly, CCITT V.24), *RS-232 Made Easy* constitutes a practical resource for a large spectrum of users. This spectrum includes users of data processing and data communication equipment, sales personnel, installers, technicians, consultants, and hobbyists who deal with all types of computer and communication systems. Although the approach is from the perspective of a microcomputer user, the systems covered range from personal computers to mainframe systems and their associated peripherals. Whatever the specifics, this book provides a single point of reference for all RS-232-related questions.

Note: Whenever RS-232 is mentioned, it refers to the latest revision of the standard, which is RS-232-C.

This work reflects the author's views only, not those of American Bell.

Special thanks is given to all the vendors listed in Appendixes F and G who provided the information necessary to compile the charts for this book.

M. D. Seyer

---

*NEC Spinwriter is a trademark of NEC Home Electronics.
†IBM PC is a trademark of International Business Machines.

RS-232
Made Easy

1

Introduction to RS-232

So, you finally decided to take the plunge! After all those trips to computer stores, many sleepless nights, and perhaps a signature loan or two, your microcomputer is no longer just a dream. You own a computer.

Proudly, you carry your latest toy home. Hurriedly, you unpack it. Nestled between pieces of cardboard and styrofoam peanuts lies the magic box of plastic, metal, and wires. Excitement and anticipation cause you to ignore your peers, parents, spouse, or progeny hollering in the background. You pull and tug. A sigh of relief escapes you as you lift the new computer from the box and find that it has no broken parts. Technocrat that you are, or assume you are, you debate whether or not to follow the assembly instructions. After coming to your senses and letting your pocketbook override your ego, you proceed to read the step-by-step procedures for device assembly. The instructions are outlined something like this:

1. Pop the top.
2. Scrape off the tape.
3. Guard the cards.
4. Put what you got in the slot.
5. Attach the cord to the mother board.
6. Label the cable.
7. Make sure the drive is alive.
8. Don't be sloppy with the floppy.
9. Twitch the switch.
10. Load the code. . . .

Booting the disk, you display the directory for a catalog of available programs. If you're lucky, a game or two will be on the disk and save you a few quarters at the arcades. But more important, you get a feel for the machine's capabilities as your proceed to bang away at the keyboard. You grudgingly scan or read the tutorial manuals that were included with your system. You may even go so far as testing your skills at some Basic-language programming. Being a novice, the extent of your programming is loop counting from 1 to 100, adding and subtracting, printing your name on the screen 100 times, tweaking the speaker, or perhaps performing some simple graphics tricks such as drawing lines or randomly displaying dots on the screen.

After many lines of ''successful'' coding, you recognize that the box truly can do more than you can convince it to do. Yes, not only can this device be used to satisfy entertainment needs, but the literature indicates that it can also serve as a business tool.

For example, a professor may have purchased the system to keep track of students' grades, attendance records, major subjects, and other information. A review of computer periodicals discloses that a large number of filing-system programs exist to satisfy this need. An example is dBASE II,* which provides an orderly means of computerizing your manual filing system. By entering the different records into the database management system, different reports may be generated—and printed, if a printer can be attached.

What about the financial wizards, such as brokers, accountants, investors, and bankers, who need quickly to calculate and recalculate figures and projections? "What if" questions have never been more easily answered than with the different spreadsheets available today. A program such as VisiCalc† can save countless hours of pencil scribblings and erasures.

An author or clerical person can hardly survive these days unless some type of word processor is utilized. The editing features allow for mistakes to be corrected prior to printing. The letter-quality printer works extremely well, with no loss of text, when properly interfaced and optioned.

How about the terminal user who has a modem or an acoustic coupler connected to the terminal or microcomputer emulating a terminal? Miles or blocks away is a computer containing a variety of information just waiting to be accessed. A service bureau, such as the Dow Jones NEWS/RETRIEVAL databank or G.E. Tymshare systems can be accessed by terminals or computers with modems, properly optioned, supporting serial communications through an RS-232 port.

Whatever the situation, as you read through the supporting documentation provided with the system, you note continual references to computers, printers, plotters, and modems that employ serial interfaces conforming to the RS-232-C standard. The documentation indicates that an expanded set of functions is available to the user if the computer or terminal supports this interface.

You quickly grab your manuals and skim through the table of contents to find the section on input/output. Your eyes light up when you reach the paragraph that confirms that your computer or terminal has an RS-232-C port or allows a circuit board to be installed that gives you this capability. Even though you know that RS-232-C is available, you still don't know whether it is a cable, a piece of software, a circuit board, or a connector.

Further reading points out the existence of 25 pins, control leads, connectors, and other components. So you ask again, "What is RS-232?" Very simply, it is pins, connectors, control signals, timing signals, data signals, ground signals, and many other things. Simplicity has just become complexity. Wouldn't things be nice if we could make things simple again? Perhaps an analogy will help.

Let's first review what RS-232 is as outlined by the formal definition of the standard. The EIA standard, RS-232-C, is the interface between data terminal equipment (DTE, typically a computer or computer terminal) and data communication equipment (DCE, typically a modem), employing serial binary data interchange. As the definition states, RS-232-C is simply a standard. This standard

---

*dBASE II is a trademark of Ashton-Tate.

†VisiCalc is a trademark of VisiCorp.

outlines the set of rules for exchanging data between business machines. These business machines can be terminals, printers, front-end processors, computers, or other equipment employing serial communications.

Why is there a need for a standard anyway? "Once upon a time," computers and terminals tried to exchange data. These business machines were usually located in different cities or buildings. However, due to their remoteness, a problem existed because one machine didn't know when to transmit characters and expect the receiving machine to get the data. Also, the characters, if not sent at the correct time, would become garbled and subsequently lost. If the characters were sent at the wrong rate of speed, bigger problems occurred. Due to the multitude of vendors supplying the business machines, different connectors came into use. When two business machines, such as a computer and printer or a terminal and modem, were to be connected, they couldn't be physically plugged together. The size and shape of the plugs were not the same. One might say that they were not "plug-compatible." It is hard to fit a square peg into a round hole. Electrical incompatibilities were also a risk. It was a "shocking" experience to connect the wrong electrical signals. These problems exemplify the need for a standard to outline the control of when, where, and how the data were to be transferred between machines.

This could easily be equated to a train attempting to cross a body of water over a drawbridge. If the bridge is drawn, the train would plunge into the water. Should this occur, all cargo on the train would be lost. Should the train be on the wrong track, a head-on collision with an oncoming rain could occur, causing havoc for both the dispatcher and receiver of the train. Another problem occurs if the train is on the wrong track. This could cause the train to miss the station it is trying to reach. The proper speed of travel should also be maintained for smooth operation on the railway system.

Wouldn't life be simpler if the track were in place and the train were on the right track, obeying the speed limit? If all these factors were tended to, the clerk at the destination depot would know when to expect the train, and the train would more than likely arrive at the station as planned.

It is obvious that without a standard set of rules for all trains to follow, transfer of cargo would not be an easy task. If the analogy is applied to our problem of business machines communicating to exchange data, you can begin to understand why the RS-232 standard was needed. Instead of manufacturers building their own unique railroads, a system standard could be established that everyone could follow. If properly adhered to, easy flow of trains could occur. This is the railway system that this book uses to describe the standard that RS-232-C represents. It provides a thorough description and understanding of what RS-232 is, as well as a detailed functional insight into the components and their interrelationships. The railway analogy is intended to provide both a layman's understanding and a technician's resource. Once the analogy is understood the reader will have obtained a working knowledge of the concepts of an RS-232 interface.

But first, let us establish a framework for the communication terminology frequently used in serial communications.

2

Communication

Jargon

This chapter describes data communication terms. If you have a good understanding of such terminology, you may skip this chapter. Recognition of the terms and acronyms presented here is important, as they are very common in the industry today. Although they are not unique to RS-232, their relevance to the RS-232 standard should be understood. The heading **Data communications** introduces technical communication definitions. These terms can easily be related to various components of the railway system mentioned in Chapter 1. Expressed in this fashion, the communication jargon will quickly become a part of your vocabulary. So, without further delay, let us get on track and start rolling!

Railroads have been exciting to people of all ages. They have been in operation for many years, yet rarely does a train crash or derail. This is even more significant when you consider that trains manage to travel in both directions on a single track without catastrophes. Sometimes there are two sets of tracks, which resolves many potential problems, but numerous single-rail systems still exist today.

What about the trains themselves? Most of them have an engine and a caboose, with the railroad cars between them. It is not uncommon to see trains with several engines and cabooses surrounding the cars. The makeup of the train plays an important role in our analogy, as you will see later.

The prerequisite for a train traveling between stations, or depots, is the construction of a railway system. There are three modes of operation on this system. The following paragraphs outline the way in which these rails can be laid.

The first case is where trains are going to be traveling in one direction only—north to south, for example. One set of rails will usually suffice. With this single track, the train can then only be traveling southbound at any time, as in Figure 2-1.

Data communications: The communication term for this mode is *simplex*. The set of rails (or, in our case, telephone lines) allowing a single direction of

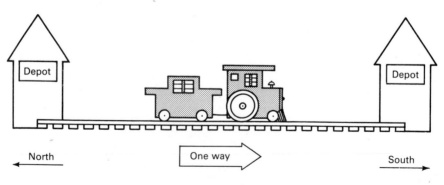

Figure 2-1

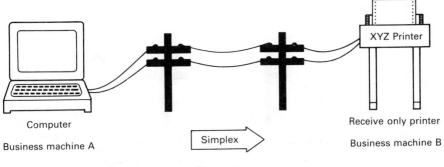

Computer

Business machine A

Simplex

Receive only printer

Business machine B

Figure 2-2

traffic can be obtained from Ma Rail (Ma Bell) or any other provider of these systems. The providers of telephone lines are commonly referred to as *common carriers*. The pair of rails in our scenario corresponds to a telephone line that is simply a pair of wires. Characters are to be transmitted only from business machine A to business machine B over these lines, as pictured in Figure 2-2. The reverse direction is not allowed in a simplex environment. *Simplex* can now be described as a mode allowing transmission of data in one direction only. This is usually accomplished by using a two-wire facility.

The second type of railway system can be constructed when trains need to travel in both directions, north and south. A single track can still handle the traffic. However, only one train can travel across the rails in a given direction at any given time (nonsimultaneously). Otherwise, a northbound train and a southbound train would collide, causing a derailment. So, train traffic can be either northbound or southbound, but not both simultaneously, as shown in Figure 2-3.

Data communications: The term for this arrangement is *half-duplex,* or *HDX*. Characters may be transmitted in both directions, but not simultaneously, over a single pair of wires, as shown in Figure 2-4. This is also known as two-way

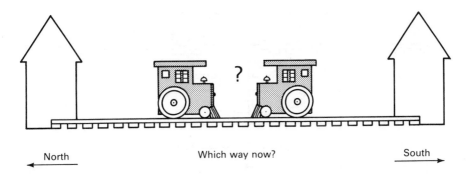

North

Which way now?

South

Figure 2-3

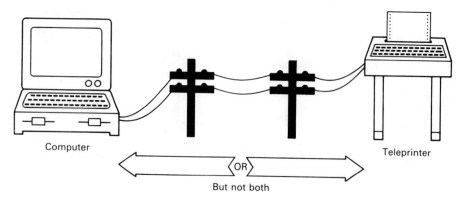

Figure 2-4

alternate transmission. The direction of traffic is alternated to utilize the single pair of wires efficiently.

Sometimes we want both northbound and southbound trains to be able to use the tracks at the same time. This is the stipulation for our third type of railway system. There are two ways of meeting this requirement. A two-track railway system can be built, with one track for northbound trains, and the other for southbound traffic. This system allows trains to travel in both directions simultaneously. The use of separate tracks eliminates the possibility of head-on collisions (Figure 2-5).

Data communications: The term for this transmission mode is *full-duplex,* or *FDX*. Characters can be transmitted in both directions, simultaneously, on a four-wire facility (two sets of tracks require four rails).

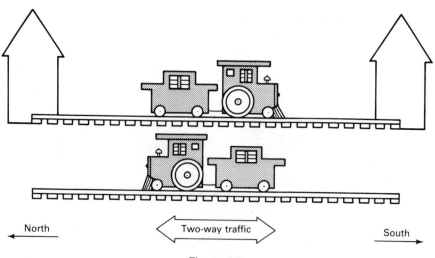

Figure 2-5

The only problem with this railway system is that the cost of buying or building the tracks can be very expensive. With a two-track system, more resources are required. The more rails the crew has to spike to the railroad ties, the greater the cost of the system for depot interconnections. Maybe this is what the common carriers are referring to when they warn that "spikes on the lines are costly"? Actually spikes on the lines are unwanted noises that cause errors in the data streams being transmitted. Usually, a retransmission of the errored data is required.

There is a way to allow data to be transmitted in both directions, simultaneously, on a two-wire facility. Because explanation of this technique is beyond the scope of this book, you are encouraged to refer to *Technical Aspects of Data Communications** by John E. McNamara for an explanation of FDX transmission over two-wire facilities.

We have described the requirements for three different railway systems that allow trains to travel between depots. It is important to realize that up to this point we haven't physically connected the depots; we have merely outlined the construction requirements. Later in this discussion we describe how we actually establish the connection of the depots that are separated by a body of water.

Data communications: *Simplex, HDX, FDX,* and *two-* or *four-wire facilities* relate to the communication modes available through the *common carrier* or telephone networks. The actual types of telephone connections are discussed in greater detail when we outline the procedures for connecting two business machines (or depots).

The goal of our train (character) is to get from station to station (business machine to business machine). These business machines could range from computers or printers to terminals. They are commonly referred to as data terminal equipment (DTE). Between the stations (DTEs) lies a body of water. To allow the trains to travel between stations, the railway system must be established. A decision must be made regarding a permanent or temporary system across the water. This decision is based on the projected number of trains that are expected to cross the water.

If the anticipated traffic load is rather large, we may elect to build a permanent railway structure across the water. The projected heavy traffic loads require that these rails be of good quality and available at all times. Generally, the quality of these tracks is proportional to their cost. The primary advantage of a permanent railway bridge is its full-time availability. The owner has use of the facility 24 hours a day.

Data communications: The technical term for our permanent railway system, or bridge, is a *private line*. Private lines, often called dedicated lines, are generally contracted for on a monthly basis from the different common carriers. The 24-hour availability of these lines allows transmission of large quantities of characters.

*Bedford, Mass.: Digital Press, 1978.

Often, the traffic volume isn't great enough to dictate the need for a permanent structure across the water. In this case, a temporary structure is available: A drawbridge will be accessible by each train station for use as needed. When trains need to cross the water, a connection is established between stations by lowering the drawbridge. This connection is broken by raising the bridge after all trains have crossed. The drawbridge will then be available to other trains. This setup is attractive because the stations pay for the use of the bridge only while it is lowered. Thus, if anticipated traffic volumes are low, a temporary facility should be considered.

Data communications: This drawbridge corresponds to the *dial-up* or *switched lines* that can be used to connect two business machines (DTEs). A call is placed between business machines using the normal telephone network and maintained as long as required for all characters to be transmitted. Upon completion, the connection is broken by hanging up the phones.

Data communications: Thus, data can be transmitted over *dial-up* or *private-line* facilities.

Both of these facilities (bridges) pass through the phone companies' switches, or central offices. These facilities are sometimes referenced as *data communication equipment* (*DCE*). The major component of DCE is a *modem*. The word *modem* is a contraction of *modulator-demodulator*. A modem is a unit incorporating a technique for placing and receiving computer signals over the common carriers' communication facility.

These modems should be viewed in our analogy as booths where traffic dispatchers, or patrolmen, reside. There is a booth at both the origination and destination locations. The dispatcher at the originating booth directs trains onto the tracks of the bridge to allow them to cross the water; the dispatcher at the far-end booth transfers the trains from the bridge to the train station.

The dispatchers also let the depots know if the bridge is available, and sometimes they provide the speed limit at which the trains can travel. The smooth operation of trains between station and dispatcher is accomplished by using common signals. Both the station and dispatcher must have a set of signals that they can generate and recognize to know when the trains can depart or arrive. The signals used to control this traffic are the major topics of the subsequent chapters of this book.

Having established that the railway system can be built in several ways and with different modes of operation, let us explore what the trains consist of and their role in our analogy. The trains are important due to the fact that they contain the cargo. After all, the cargo dictated the need for the railway system in the first place.

In order for cargo to be shipped from one location to another (depot to depot), certain types of railroad cars are needed. The most common cars used today are boxcars and flatcars. We will use these in our comparison.

At the depot, the train is put together with a combination of boxcars and flatcars. The number of cars allowed per train varies between depots. This variance

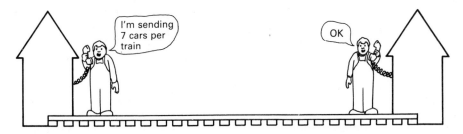

Figure 2-6

causes problems when cargo is to be shipped on these cars to another depot. The receiving depot, not knowing the number of cars to expect, will never know if the entire shipment was received. So the originator must notify the destination depot of the makeup and number of cars in the train. Knowing this, the destination depot can determine if the number of cars that arrived is the same as the number sent (Figure 2-6).

Data communications: The selection of boxcars and flatcars was intentional. These two car types allow a graphic representation of characters that business machines transmit. A character can be viewed as a specific number of 1s and 0s. The specific number of 1s and 0s representing characters is established by the machine manufacturers. Whether they be terminals, printers, or computers, this number must be consistent at both ends before data can be exchanged between two devices. Typically, these 1s and 0s are viewed as representing two positions, on and off. Pictorially, Figure 2-7 could represent a character.

Understanding what particular character these 1s and 0s represent is not important for now. There exist character code sets that determine the specific makeup of any given character. One of the most prominent is ASCII. Any given set of 1s and 0s represents a specific character. Character makeup can be derived from available ASCII charts. The important point to note is that each 1 and 0 makes up a tiny bit of the whole character. For ease of reference, we will call them *bits,* which just happens to be official name for them, though this word *bit* originated as a contraction of "binary digit."

If we assume that a boxcar is a 1 bit and the flatcar is a 0 bit, our picture would be very much the same as before (Figure 2-8).

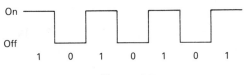

Figure 2-7

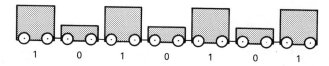

Figure 2-8

Data communications: The following discussion is unique to a communication technique termed *asynchronous transmission,* also known as *start/stop
transmission.*

A train would not be complete without an engine and a caboose. When you
see an engine coming down the track, you know that railroad cars are close behind.
This engine signifies the beginning of the train. In our example, the engine would be
followed by the specific number of boxcars and flatcars previously discussed. To
signify the end of the train, a caboose is attached. The next trains will consist of the
same engine-cars-caboose sequence. Often, more than one caboose and engine are
attached. But for simplicity, we only will use one engine and one caboose per train,
as in Figure 2-9.

Data communications: In technical terms, the engine, which signifies
the beginning of the train, represents what is known as a *start bit.* The start bit in-
forms the business machine that data bits (boxcars and flatcars) will follow. After
the data bits, a caboose is attached to indicate the end of the character. This caboose
is termed a *stop bit.* As you can see in Figures 2-10 and 2-11, our train (or *character*) consists of a *start bit, data bits,* and a *stop bit,* which correspond to our engine-
boxcar/flatcar-caboose sequence.

Figure 2-9

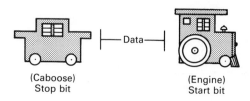

(Caboose)   (Engine)
Stop bit   Start bit

Figure 2-10

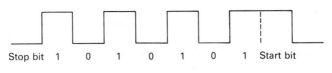

Stop bit   1   0   1   0   1   0   1   Start bit

Figure 2-11

Data communications: The fact that the stop bit may or may not be at the same level as the last bit of the character is not important. Simply keep in mind that the stop bit is a unique bit that trails the data bits.

What happens if the wrong type of cars is used in a train, if boxcars are used instead of flatcars? How does the destination depot know that some of the cars are wrong? The problem could be resolved in the following fashion: No matter how many boxcars are in the train, there should always be an odd number of boxcars. In reality, railroad cars are not arbitrarily added to keep the train to a consistent length. But, for ease of understanding, we will assume this in the analogy. The goal is to permit the depot at the destination to confirm that the proper railroad cars were received. The originator of the train makes this possible simply by counting the number of boxcars in the train. If it is an even number, the engineer adds another boxcar, making the number odd. If the number is odd, the engineer adds a flatcar. These actions not only keep the number of boxcars odd but also keep the trains the same length. As long as the receiving depot (computer or terminal) knows that an odd number of boxcars is supposed to arrive, a count can be made to determine if the correct train arrived at the depot. If the boxcar count is an even number at the final destination, the receiving depot knows that the correct cars were not received (Figure 2-12).

Data communications: This concept of keeping an odd number of bits (boxcars) in a character (train) is known as *parity*. The boxcar or flatcar that was added to keep the number odd is known as the *parity bit*. By counting the number of 1s (boxcars), the receiving depot does a *parity check*. If the number of 1 bits is even

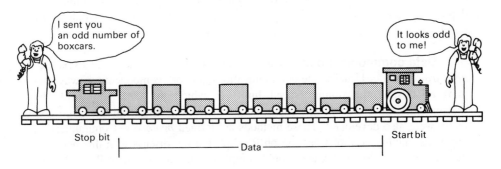

Figure 2-12

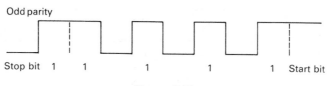

Figure 2-13

a *parity error* has occurred, making the received character incorrect. The causes of parity errors are numerous, some of the more common causes being poor-quality communication lines, power surges, and poor interface connections. Any of these conditions may cause the flipping of one of the character's bits as it travels over the communication facility. A similar scheme could just as easily have been chosen to check for an even number of 1s. This is how the terms *odd* and *even parity* came into existence (Figure 2-13).

Data communications: The concept of enclosing a character with a *start* and *stop bit* is known as *asynchronous transmission*. The start bit (engine) indicates to the receiving depot the time to start looking for the cars of the train; the stop bit (caboose) lets the depot know when the entire train had arrived. The "timing" for the beginning and end of the train is provided by the engine and caboose. Because of this, it is said that, in asynchronous transmission, the start and stop bits provide the *timing*. Each character (train) is individually *synchronized* (timed).

As the need for shipping more cargo came about, more trains were needed. However, the existing railway system wasn't adequate for these trains. What was needed was a railway system that allowed both longer and faster trains. Also, operational costs skyrocketed because one engine and one caboose were required for every train (character). Valuable time on the track was being wasted for engines and cabooses when it could have been used for more boxcars and flatcars.

So, the railway system was improved to allow faster trains and to provide a means of combining little trains into larger trains. This reduced the number of engines and cabooses required, freeing up more track time. Because of the increased speeds and sizes of the trains, a speed limit was needed for safety purposes. The decision was made to allow the railway system to establish the speed limit. The depots agreed to abide by this limit. If properly adhered to, the depots would know exactly how fast the longer trains should be traveling (Figure 2-14).

Data communications: This transmission scheme is known as *synchronous transmission*. Usually, the communications network component (railway system) established the timing (speed limit) at which the data bits would be transmitted. Better methods of determining whether the data (trains) arrived correctly were also developed. These methods are termed *protocols*. Communication protocols, having no direct bearing on RS-232, are not discussed in this book, as they are extremely complex and would complicate the discussion of RS-232. Furthermore, because the bulk of microcomputers and terminals in the market today use

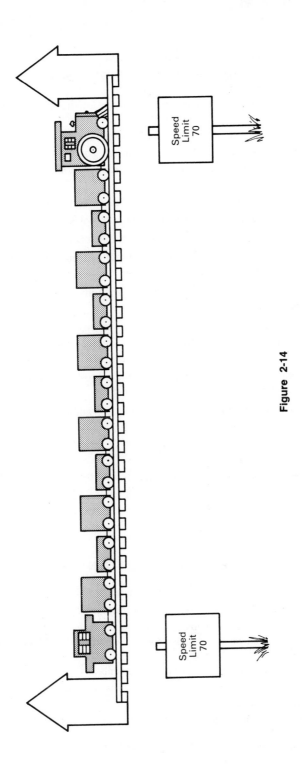

Figure 2-14

low speeds or unsophisticated protocols, we have chosen to concentrate on asynchronous transmission environments. However, synchronous transmission will be discussed again when the timing elements of RS-232 are explained. Elsewhere, unless specifically mentioned, you can assume that we are discussing an asynchronous environment.

At this point, you should have a general understanding of the *format* and *timing* of *characters* in an *asynchronous* environment. The following is a quick review of our analogy as it relates to data communication jargon.

1. The railroad tracks are the telephone lines or communication facilities.
2. *Data* transmission occurs when the trains travel along the tracks.
3. Tracks allowing trains to go in one direction only are termed *simplex*.
4. Tracks allowing train traffic in both directions but not simultaneously are termed *half-duplex,* or *HDX*.
5. Tracks allowing tracks to travel in both directions simultaneously are referred to as *full-duplex,* or *FDX*.
6. *Asynchronous transmission* takes place in an environment in which *characters* (boxcars and flatcars) have a *start bit* (engine) and a *stop bit* (caboose) to indicate the beginning and end of the *data bits*.
7. *Data terminal equipment (DTE)* is considered to be computers, terminals, or printers — depots and stations in our analogy.
8. *Data communication equipment (DCE)* is considered to be the *modems* between the computers, terminals, and printers — denoted as booths in our analogy.

Although these terms are not unique to RS-232, their understanding is a prerequisite to a true comprehension of the need for and operation of the RS-232 interface in a communication environment. Now that you are on track, let's proceed on down the rails. All aboard!

REVIEW QUESTIONS*

1. A mode of transmission in which each character is individually timed is _____.
2. _____ facilities allow transmission in one direction only.
3. The distinction between half-duplex and full-duplex is that HDX allows traffic in both directions nonsimultaneously/simultaneously, while FDX allows two-way traffic nonsimultaneously/simultaneously.
4. Common carriers provide _____ for data transmission.
5. A business machine can be one of many devices. List three of the most prevalent: _____, _____, _____.
6. DTE, potentially either terminals, printers, or computers, is the acronym for _____.

*Answers to Review Questions will be found in Chapter 9.

7. DCE, generally modems, is the acronym for _____.

8. The _____ interface is the interface between DTE and DCE employing serial binary data interchange.

9. A type of line that is only temporary in nature is called a _____ line.

10. _____ lines are used when traffic volume between two locations is extremely high.

11. _____ is the contraction for <u>modulator-demodulator</u>.

12. A _____ converts computer signals for transmission over the common carriers' communication facilities.

13. _____ are used to control the exchange of data between DTE and DCE.

14. The scheme of counting the number of bits in a character to determine whether it is odd or even is known as _____.

15. The bits surrounding the data bits of a character are the _____ and _____ bits.

3

Asynchronous Modems and RS-232-C

With a general understanding of some basic communication terminology, we are ready for a detailed explanation of the specifics of the RS-232-C interface. This will be accomplished by building upon our basic railway system analogy. At the end of this chapter is a summary of the railway system and its corresponding communication-environment counterparts.

The function of RS-232-interface leads depends on the type of communication facility used, dial-up or private lines. This chapter focuses on a dial-up environment.

In what areas would a dial-up environment be appropriate? A dial-up connection is normally used, for example, to access a database service, such as The Source.* The information available from The Source, such as commodity and stock quotes, is to be shared by a large terminal or computer population. Typically, access to the service is for short periods of time. For example, a user may desire a small report once each day from the service. Over a dial-up facility, the user connects to a port, retrieves the information, logs off, and then disconnects from the port. The port is now available for other users to access. Dial-up facilities fit nicely where there are low traffic volumes per user. Many different dial-up facilities, such as Telenet† and TYMNET,‡ are available for accessing the different services. Charges for these access services generally are per minute. The cost of these facilities in conjunction with traffic volumes determines when dial-up lines are more economical than other facilities, such as private lines. These two major factors influence the use of dial-up connections in the following types of service offerings:

1. Public databases
2. Service bureaus
3. Message services
4. Computer-to-computer data exchanges

These are but a few of the many areas in which RS-232-C is used in a dial-up environment, but they are the ones covered in this chapter.

In our treatment of the interactions of RS-232-C leads, the train depots correspond to our computer, terminals, or printers (DTE) and the booths to our modems (DCE). These leads are separated by category, such as data, control, ground, and timing, for ease of learning. Our discussion begins with the data leads necessary for transmitting information.

*The Source is a service mark of Source Telecomputing Corp.
†Telenet is a service mark of GTE Corp.
‡TYMNET is a service mark of G.E. Co.

A dispatcher knows that there are two kinds of trains at a depot, departing and arriving trains. Departing trains have a preassigned track, say, track 2. All leaving trains will depart on this track.

Once they cross the water and reach the far-end toll booth, the trains are switched to a different track, track 3, which is set aside for arriving trains. The dispatcher, by assigning separate tracks, can monitor each and see if any trains are departing to or arriving from the booths and drawbridge.

RS-232:   In an RS-232 environment, the departing trains are the *transmitted data,* and the arriving trains are the *received data.* All data (trains) departing from the station (business machine) will go across a track called the *transmitted data lead.* A track (lead), known as the *received data lead,* is set aside for all arriving trains (data) to use. In an RS-232-C interface, 25 *pins,* or leads, are available for use by the DTE and DCE (see Figure A-1). However, only a limited number of leads are used as "tracks" for data transfer. Each lead has a preassigned function. For example, the transmitted data go across pin 2, whereas the received data arrive on pin 3. By monitoring pin 2, transmitted data can be detected. To check if data are being received, pin 3 should be monitored. The tools available to monitor these and other leads are discussed in Appendix E.

Keep in mind that at one end of the track, the train is considered to be departing, but once it crosses the bridge, it is considered an arriving train at the destination depot.

RS-232:   Transmitted data at the originating DTE are on pin 2 of the *RS-232 interface,* whereas, at the receiving DTE, these same data arrive on pin 3, as shown in Figure 3-1. Transmitted data are "output" at one end and become "input" at the other end.

For example, when a terminal is connected to The Source, the keyboard operator's typed characters are passed from the terminal to the modem on pin 2. These

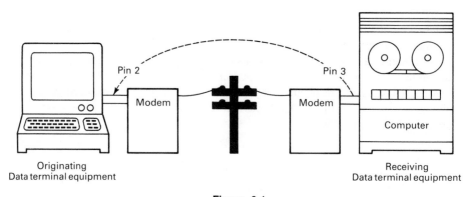

Originating
Data terminal equipment   Receiving
                                                           Data terminal equipment

Figure 3-1

output data are transmitted over the communication line to the far-end modem. At this end, the received data are presented to the computer as input on pin 3.

Our bridge is a drawbridge. Control of the tracks must be maintained. The depot (DTE) must know when the bridge is in place. The booth attendant must inform the dispatcher at the station when the train (data) can be moved (transmitted) over the bridge (communication facilities). To keep our trains from going into the deep, the drawbridge had better be lowered between the two depots when each train reaches it. Lowering the drawbridge corresponds to establishing a telephone connection between DTE locations.

As a train approaches the water, it must let the other depot know that the bridge must be lowered. Each train station is equipped with a bell that produces a loud ring. Let's set up a procedure for indicating when to lower the bridge. Whenever a booth (modem) hears the ringing from the distant station, this should be interpreted as an indication that the bridge should be lowered. We will call this our *ring indicator*. The scenario would be similar to Figure 3-2.

RS-232:   In the actual RS-232 interface, pin 22 is known as the *ring indicator*. When the number of the telephone associated with a modem is dialed, this lead will indicate that ringing is occurring. It will go on and off in direct correlation with the phone rings. This is an indication that a request is being made for establishment of a dial-up connection.

The booth operator at the distant end hears the ringing. However, he doesn't want to lower the bridge for the train to arrive unless he knows for certain that there is someone at the depot ready to receive the train. If the train arrived while the depot was not being operated, no one could receive and inspect it, and the train could get lost in the railroad yard. So, as a rule, the booth will not lower the bridge unless the station is manned.

RS-232:   This signal from the depot (DTE) is termed *data terminal ready (DTR)*. Pin 20 is a control lead or signal used by the DTE to indicate that the modem

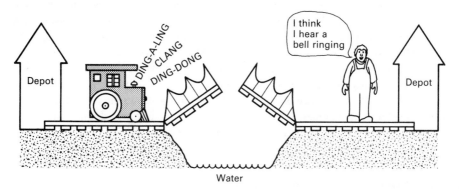

Figure 3-2

should answer the phone. Some modems are equipped with the capability to answer the call automatically if pin 20 is on. This feature, termed *auto-answer,* allows for terminal users to establish a telephone connection with an unmanned computer site. Although not an RS-232-C term, *auto-answer* utilizes pins on the RS-232 interface. Generally, if the machine's power is on, DTR will be on, enabling calls to be answered for the connection to be established.

Let's assume that the train station is manned by someone who turns on a light when a request is received to signal that the booth attendant should lower the bridge. When the booth operator hears the bell ringing, he lowers his half of the bridge.

At the originating station, the booth operator can tell that the remote operator has lowered his part of the bridge. He checks to see if his end should be lowered in the same fashion. If his station has given him the proper signal, he lowers the bridge. If the station failed to pass him the signal, he refuses to lower the bridge. The far-end booth operator waits to see if the bridge was actually lowered. If the bridge was not lowered, after a period of time, the operator raises his end so that other trains might have access to the bridge.

RS-232:   This is referred to as *timing out.* Timing out occurs if the proper signal (DTR) is not present at one of the ends. The *communication path* will not be established. However, if the DTR signals are present at both ends, the connection is maintained. To disconnect a dial-up connection, either end merely drops DTR (pin 20).

Generally, most commercially available databases, time-sharing systems, and other services are set up to support auto-answer. This allows for unattended operation of the service. For example, to access Dow Jones services, you merely dial the phone number of a port on the computer. Because the port is optioned for auto-answer, DTR will be on, allowing the modem to answer the call automatically. By answering the call, the modem returns a high-pitched answer-back tone to the originator. Upon detection of this tone, the originator enters data mode manually, or automatically if the modem can accomplish this, completing the connection. DTR determines if the connection is maintained or not.

Some modems offer auto-dial capabilities. If these types of modems are used, the phone number can be dialed automatically. Upon detection of the answer-back tone, the modem automatically completes the connection without human intervention. The Hayes Smartmodem* and Ven-Tel MD212 Plus† are two such modems. The Ven-Tel, for example, allows either keyboard entry of a phone number or a selection of prestored numbers to be dialed. This is accomplished without the need for a telephone handset. The presence of DTR (pin 20) allows the connections to be established and maintained. If the far-end computer or terminal doesn't have DTR on, the modem will not answer the call. In the case of auto-dialers, the ringing will

---

*Smartmodem is a trademark of Hayes Microcomputer Products.

†MD212 Plus is a trademark of Ven-Tel Inc.

continue forever unless intelligence is added. The originating modem should monitor the number of rings and abort the call after a preset number of unsuccessful rings. The intelligence in the modem could allow for an alternate number or numbers to be called if a "no answer" condition occurs.

If the dialed number is busy, the modem can retry the call until a successful connection is made. Features such as auto-dial, storing numbers, and counting the number of rings are made possible by putting intelligence, generally microprocessors, into the modems.

This intelligence has to be able to monitor the obvious signal of DTR, pin 20, but also has to take into account previously discussed RS-232 signals. For example, the number to be called, input on the keyboard of the terminal or computer, must be transmitted from the terminal or computer to the modem. This number, output on pin 2 (transmitted data), must be recognized by the modem as a digit to be dialed. The modem must know when all of the digits are received to make a valid call. Usually, the terminal operator ends the number with a carriage return, which serves as a delimiter indicating that the modem should dial that number. These digits from the terminal are standard ASCII representations of numbers. The modem must translate the ASCII characters into dial pulses or Touch-Tone* digits that the standard phone network can understand. This is because the telephone network has no way of knowing whether a machine or a human is placing a call. It only knows Touch-Tone or rotary-dialed pulses.

How does an "intelligent" modem indicate that a busy condition, no answer, some other problem, or a successful call has occurred? Recall that the terminal or computer receives its characters on pin 3, received data, over the RS-232-C interface. The modem must interpret the condition and pass the appropriate message to the terminal on pin 3.

Once the call setup has taken place, the intelligence of the modem must become almost transparent and allow the modem to behave like the standard asynchronous modem. In this mode, modulation and demodulation of the character take place as discussed in Chapter 2. The RS-232-C signals now are used according to the standard.

Assume that the bridge is successfully lowered to allow trains across. To let each depot know this, each booth gives a signal to the depots indicating that the bridge is lowered.

RS-232:   The term for this lead is *data set ready (DSR)*. This signal is on pin 6. In a dial-up environment, DSR is asserted to the proper voltage, that is, goes high, if a communication path has been established.

RS-232:   The telephone connection is now established. Here is a quick review of the sequence of events.

*Touch-Tone is a trademark of AT&T.

1. The phone number is dialed.
2. *Ring indicator* (pin 22) is on at the distant end.
3. If the terminal or computer is on, DTR is on, allowing the call to be answered. This is termed *auto-answer*. When DTR is on and *ring indicator* is detected, the call will be automatically answered.
4. Once answered, each *modem* will raise its *data set ready* lead as an indication that a line is present for that station.
5. The originating station is on; its DTR lead is on (high), so the connection can be maintained. Usually, if a terminal is involved in originating the call, a data button on the phone must be pushed to maintain the connection.
6. The connection is now established.
7. Data may now be exchanged between the two devices.

When the transfer of information is completed, the connection is broken when either end drops DTR. The terminal operator may drop DTR generally in one of three ways:

1. Manually disconnect (hang up) the call.
2. Place the terminal into a mode known as "local mode." This is contrasted with being "on-line." While in on-line mode, DTR is on. By placing the terminal off-line or in local mode, DTR is lowered, automatically causing the modem to drop the connection.
3. Unplugging or turning off the terminal or computer. Lack of power lowers DTR, causing a disconnect by the modem.

The far-end computer can also generally break the connection in one of several ways:

1. If someone unplugs the computer (heaven forbid!), DTR will go off, causing the modem to hang up.
2. The program executing in the computer can generally control the DTR signal and bring it down at will.
3. Often, the unit handling the communications for the computer, known as a front-end processor (FEP), can recognize a disconnect character from the far-end terminal or computer. Generally, in an asynchronous environment, a Control-D character sequence will be received and interpreted by the host computer or FEP as a disconnect sequence. Once this sequence is received, the FEP will drop DTR, causing the modem to disconnect.

Data terminal ready plays a major role in the establishment, maintenance, and disconnecting of a dial-up connection.

For now, let's keep DTR on to maintain the line. So far, the train is right on schedule. Several types of railway systems have been discussed. One-track, one-way (simplex); one-track, two-way, nonsimultaneous (half-duplex); and one- or two-track, two-way, simultaneous (full-duplex) paths were explained in Chapter 2. For now, ignore the simplex and FDX facilities for transmitting data; we are going to focus on half-duplex (HDX).

In this mode, the bridge across the water has only one set of tracks. Things could really get messy if we didn't control when and in which direction each train would cross the bridge. The booth attendants must maintain control of the situation to prevent trains from colliding and ending up in the water.

The depots, with trains wanting to cross the bridge, are in contention for the right-of-way on the tracks. When they want to send the trains (data), they should turn on the engines' headlights, signaling a request to send the trains across. The headlights can be seen all the way across the water. So, if the local booth attendant sees the lights initiated by the station (DTE), he knows that the right-of-way was desired. However, the booth attendant had better check to see if the far end has the right to the track prior to giving this privilege to the local depot. Because the engine headlights are so bright, he is easily able to see if the far end had control of the track or not. If he detected a light, he would not honor the request to send (Figure 3-3). If, however, no light was detected from the far end, the booth attendant would give a clear-to-send signal to its station. The depot could send as many trains across the bridge as desired because it had control of the bridge.

Once all of the trains had crossed the bridge, the sending depot operator would turn out the headlights as an indication that he was relinquishing control of the track. Either end could then request to send trains across the bridge and be given a clear-to-send signal by the booth attendants. Obviously, the booth attendants play an important role in controlling the smoothness of operation over the railway system.

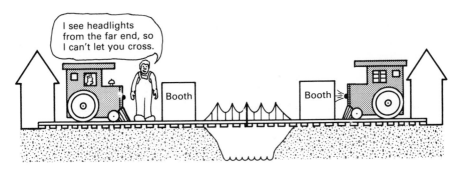

Figure 3-3

RS-232: In a half-duplex environment, contention for the communication facilities exists. A typical modem found in this class is a 202* type. The 202 is a Bell System modem type that operates in a half-duplex fashion at 1200 bits per second (bps). Modems that operate in the same environment are said to be 202-compatible or look-alikes. Control of this two-way, nonsimultaneous path is handled by a DTE-DCE interaction. DTE-1 raises a *request to send (RTS)*, pin 4, if it has data to transmit. This causes a signal to be passed across the telephone line, detectable at the other end on pin 8. The signal at the far end is termed *data carrier detect (DCD)* or *received line signal detector*. It is important to note that although separate pins are used for different functions on the interface, this does not imply that a separate communication facility for each is required. In reality, all signals are passed over the same path. Locally, however, the modem first checks its own DCD lead, pin 8. If its DCD is not on, a *clear-to-send (CTS)* signal is passed to the local DTE-1. DTE-1 now has control of the facilities and can transmit data on the proper lead (pin 2). However, if the local modem detects that pin 8 is on, a CTS signal will not be given to DTE-1. The fact that DCD is on is an indication that the far end has control of the line. Figure 3-4 pictorially represents the interaction of the leads.

The following summarizes the DTE-DCE interaction.

1. RTS (pin 4) is raised by DTE.
2. DCD (pin 8) is checked by the modem to see if the far-end DTE has its RTS high.
3. If the far end's RTS is high (DCD is on), the modem does not give CTS, and the DTE drops RTS and goes back to step 1. If DCD is off, it proceeds to step 4.
4. If DCD is off, the local modem (DCE), after a slight delay, gives a CTS (pin 5) signal to the DTE.
5. DTE then presents data on the transmitted data lead (pin 2), and the modem transmits this to the far end.
6. The receiving modem puts the received data on pin 3 for presentation to the destination DTE.
7. The originating DTE continues with RTS held high until all data are transmitted. Then it drops its RTS, which drops DCD at the far end and CTS locally, causing the line to be idle once again.
8. Either DTE can now raise RTS to obtain control of the line.

What if our bridge across the water allows two-way simultaneous traffic? We don't have to worry about who has control of the track because each station has its own path across the bridge. To save time and capitalize on our two-way concurrent traffic possibilities, the dispatchers should turn their headlights on and leave them on while the stations are manned. Thus, each booth attendant will always give his

---

*The 202 is a trademark of the Bell System.

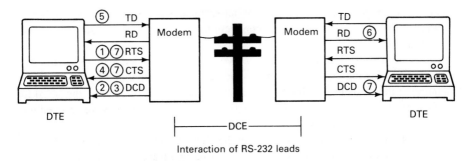

Interaction of RS-232 leads

Figure 3-4

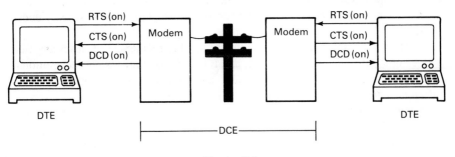

Figure 3-5

depot a clear-to-send signal, even though he detects headlights from across the bridge. Now the stations can send traffic across a bridge without worrying about obtaining the right-of-way on the bridge.

RS-232: This is termed *full-duplex*. Several modems offer full-duplex capabilities. For example, a 103J*-compatible modem operates FDX at 300 bps. A 212A* look-alike modem generally offers two speeds, 300 and 1200 bps, both available in a full-duplex mode. Both DTEs have RTS held high, both modems given CTS constantly, and both modems have DCD high because the far end's RTS lead is on constantly (Figure 3-5).

The trains are really smokin' along the tracks now. But what happens if the bridge malfunctions or the operators vacate the stations? Obviously, all traffic should cease. The booth attendant turns off his CTS signal and raises the bridge. To start traffic again, the entire procedure must be repeated.

RS-232: If DTR goes off (loses power, for instance), the modem will disconnect the line. The modem will no longer have DSR high as an indication to the

*103J and 212A are trademarks of the Bell System.

DTE that a connection is established. Whether the communication mode is HDX or FDX, the procedure for the dial-up connection will have to be repeated for further data transmission.

We have just described the role of several RS-232-C leads in a dial-up environment. Following is a review of the interface leads, separated by function. By separating the leads into distinct functions and noting their directions, the serial interface can be easily understood. This will become more evident as we proceed into areas of cross connections.

Note the last two interface leads in the chart in Figure 3-6. The *ground leads* are important for electrical reasons. Pin 1 is usually a frame ground to keep people from receiving shocks in the event of electrical shorts or problems. This is the same principle that is applied to the grounded wall outlets of your home. Pin 7 is termed *signal ground* and is used as a reference for all other signals on the interface. For example, the signal on pin 7 establishes the common ground reference potential for all the other circuits except pin 1. The function of these two leads is easily understood.

Throughout this text, abbreviations for the different RS-232-C leads are used. These acronyms, such as DTR, DSR, and RTS, are used for ease of recognition of the leads. In practice, the EIA RS-232-C and CCITT V.24 standards use totally different nomenclatures. For example, in RS-232, the categories of leads, ground, data, control, and timing are referred to as the A, B, C, and D circuits. The international standard denotes the various pins by numbers such as 101, 102, 108.2, and so on. Although these standards outline the precise labeling of the leads, the industry usually refers to them by either pin assignments, such as pin 20, or the acronyms used in this text, such as DTR. This is why only pin numbers and acronyms are used here. Refer to Appendix A (Figure A-1) for the precise circuit nomenclature, if needed.

The remainder of this chapter is devoted to the subject of modem tests. Generally, asynchronous modems offer diagnostics to the user that can aid in a quick determination of problems when they occur in a configuration. Problems are evident when the data being received or transmitted are garbled. Transmission of the data may be restricted by a faulty modem. To understand the tests available to isolate the problem, a general description of signal forms must be known. In review, the func-

Function	Pin	Lead name (abbreviation)	Direction
Data	2	Transmitted data (TD)	From DTE
Data	3	Received data (RD)	From DCE
Control	4	Request to send (RTS)	From DTE
Control	5	Clear to send (CTS)	From DCE
Control	8	Data carrier detect (DCD)	From DCE
Control	6	Data set ready (DSR)	From DCE
Control	20	Data terminal ready (DTR)	From DTE
Control	22	Ring indicator (RI)	From DCE
Ground	1	Protective ground (PG)	N/A
Ground	7	Signal ground (SG)	N/A

Figure 3-6

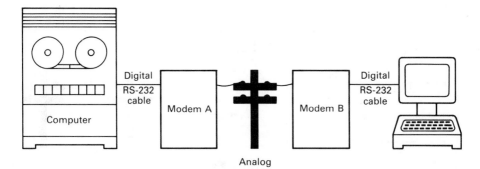

Figure 3-7

tion of a modem, when transmitting, is to convert (modulate) a digital signal from a computer, terminal, or printer onto the analog telephone network. When receiving, the purpose is to convert the received data back into their original digital form (Figure 3-7).

To perform the conversions, each modem is equipped with a transmitter and a receiver (Figure 3-8).

To determine if a modem is faulty, four tests are available: analog loopback, digital loopback, remote digital loopback, and self-test. They are generally activated by pressing buttons on the front of the modems.

Analog Loopback (AL).   If the AL button is pressed at modem A, its transmitter is looped back to its receiver as it is disconnected from the line (Figure 3-9). Anything transmitted through the modem will be immediately echoed back through the receiver. Anything output by the computer on pin 2 will be received on pin 3 (received data). This allows for testing the output and input functions on the analog side of the modem, consequently termed *analog loopback.* If the output by the computer doesn't match the input it receives by the loopback, the local modem has a problem.

Digital Loopback (DL).   If the DL button is pressed at modem A, its receiver is looped back on the RS-232 side to its transmitter (Figure 3-10). Conceptually, anything that is received by modem A from the far end (modem B)

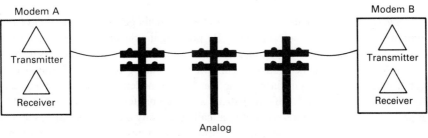

Figure 3-8

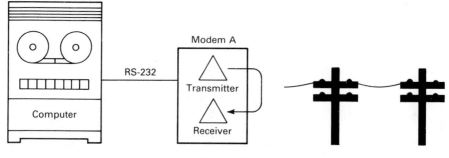

Figure 3-9

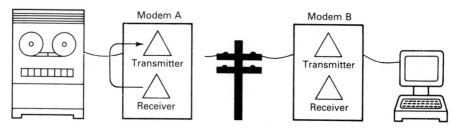

Figure 3-10

will be looped from pin 3 on the RS-232 side to pin 2 or will transmit data back to modem B. The data may never actually appear on the RS-232 pins, but the concept applies. Even though the terminal at modem B will be originating the characters to be echoed, someone must be physically present at modem A to push the DL button. From this you can see that coordination at each end is required. This test is normally done after the local modem has passed the AL test. If the results of the DL test are negative—that is, if transmitted characters are not the same as received characters—the far-end modem could have a problem.

Remote Digital Loopback (RDL).   By pressing this button, the need for the manual pressing of the DL button at the far-end modem is eliminated. If the RDL button is pressed on modem A, a signal is passed to modem B that causes it automatically to go into DL mode, functioning as previously described. This capability eliminates a lot of the coordination efforts.

Self-Test (ST).   This button relieves the terminal operator or computer of the requirement of generating a test pattern. By pressing the ST button, a test pattern is generated by the modem. Depending on the setting of the AL, DL, and RDL buttons, different sides of the modems will be tested, analog or digital. Generally, a light or other indication will flash on the front of the modem if an error is received. The difference between a self-test pattern and a computer- or terminal-generated pattern is that the electronics will automatically catch any errors. Normally, the terminal operator or computer would have to compare transmitted patterns with received patterns to determine problems.

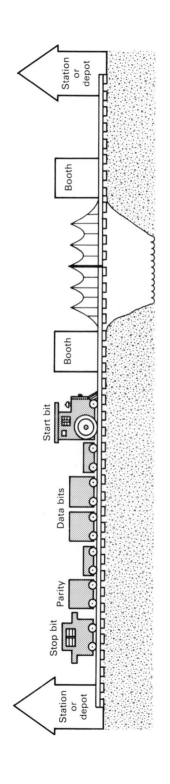

Figure 3-11 Summary of railway system analogy with communication environment equivalents.

REVIEW QUESTIONS

1. Transmitted data are found on pin _____. Once these data arrive at the other end of the facility, they are found on pin _____, known as _____.

2. The lead monitored by the DTE to determine that a call is being received is pin _____, which is _____. Will it stay on constantly? Explain.

3. If the ring indicator is detected, the lead that must be on for the modem to answer and maintain the call is pin _____, which is _____.

4. How can the DTE be assured that the connection is established?

5. If contention for the line exists, the mode of operation is _____.

6. To bid for control of a line, the DTE raises the lead on pin _____, which is _____. If the modem, (DCE) doesn't see _____ on, _____ is given to the DTE.

7. If pin 8 (DCD) is detected, what lead at the other end has been raised?

8. What lead is turned off, or dropped, to disconnect a dial-up line?

9. Protective ground is found on pin _____.

10. Signal ground is a _____ for all other signals and is found on pin _____.

11. Explain how pins 2 and 3 are used by an intelligent modem, above and beyond their normal functions.

12. A terminal can cause a disconnect from a line in a number of ways. Explain the different ways and relate them to the RS-232 pins.

13. Explain the justification for using auto-answer at a remote computer site. Explain the RS-232 significance, such as a no-answer condition. How does the modem or computer sense that a call is being received?

14. When a service bureau or time-sharing system is accessed, generally a log-on prompt occurs upon a successful connection to determine if you are a valid user. The log-on generally consists of an ID and password. How does the host computer know when to prompt the originator for the ID and password? Explain in terms of RS-232 interaction.

15. In RS-232 connections, the importance of perspective of lead direction is often overlooked. Recall that certain signals were output from the DTE, while others were output from the DCE. State a rule of thumb for lead direction and describe it in terms of DTE-DCE interaction.

16. Complete the following chart.

Function	Pin	Lead Name (Abbr.)	Direction
Data	_____	Transmitted data (TD)	_____
Data	_____	Received data (RD)	_____
Control	_____	Request to sent (_____)	_____
Control	_____	Clear to send (_____)	_____
Control	_____	Data carrier detect (_____)	_____
Control	_____	Data set ready (_____)	_____
Control	_____	Data terminal ready (_____)	_____
Control	_____	Ring indicator (_____)	From DCE
Ground	_____	Protective ground (_____)	N/A
Ground	_____	Signal ground (_____)	N/A

4

RS-232 Operation in a Private-Line Environment

Chapter 3 dealt with a temporary lowering of the drawbridge. Recall that this corresponded to a dial-up or switched-line environment in the communication business. The reason for the temporary structure is the limited traffic between train stations, as well as cost considerations.

What if traffic volume between stations increases to the point at which it is not economical to keep raising and lowering the drawbridge? The cost of raising and lowering the bridge could become greater than the cost of maintaining a permanent connection. When either high volume or high costs are typical, a permanent structure between depots should be considered.

RS-232: This arrangement is termed a *private line,* also called a *leased line*. Private lines are permanent connections between terminals, computers, or a mixture of both. Although the cost is sometimes high, these lines are available 24 hours a day for a flat monthly rate. This availability allows for greater data transmission without concern for increased cost.

Typical applications utilizing private lines are on-line data entry or inquiry-response systems with high volumes of data traffic. A terminal operator can input or retrieve data throughout the day. Typically, these applications are found on larger systems of the minicomputer or mainframe size. The higher volumes dictate higher transmission speeds, which until recently have been limited to synchronous transmission. However, technology in asynchronous transmission is evolving to allow much higher speeds than the 1200–1800-bps limitations in the past. Nonetheless, asynchronous or synchronous, the cost of private lines may be restrictive until traffic volumes reach a trade-off level, at which it becomes uneconomical to continue to use dial-up facilities. Private lines may then be justifiable.

For example, an airline reservation agent may have a terminal connected via a private line to a host computer in a distant city. Because of the large number of telephone inquiries handled by the agent daily, a dial-up connection is probably impractical. With this level of traffic, much of the time could be spent dialing and establishing the connections. Also, analysis of typical long-distance rates would indicate that after a certain number of hours each day, it becomes cheaper to procure a leased or private line. Once again, traffic volumes and costs determine whether a dial-up or private line is used.

Although most of the RS-232 signals are the same as in the dial-up environment, some of them are functionally different or not used at all. In our dial-up analogy, the first signal used was the ringing of the bell, indicating that the bridge connection should be made. In a private-line environment, no ringing indication is needed because we have a permanent bridge structure.

This also implies that the data terminal ready (DTR) signal need not interact with the ring indicator. The manned depot, in our analogy, had to turn on a light

(DTR) signaling that the bridge could be lowered. Obviously, there is no bridge lowering, so the booth operator doesn't even check for the light signal from the station.

RS-232:   *Data terminal ready* (pin 20) may be present at the DTE; however, the DCE often ignores this lead in a private-line environment.

As you can see, this cuts out almost 50 percent of our headaches. Without ring indicator (pin 22), and with data terminal ready (pin 20) at both ends, we need only concern ourselves with the data leads (pins 2 and 3), the ground leads (pins 1 and 7), and the remaining control leads: request to send (pin 4), clear to send (pin 5), data set ready (pin 6), and data carrier detect (pin 8). The data and ground leads function in the same manner in either a private-line or dial-up environment, so we won't repeat them.

With a permanent bridge across the water, we have only to make sure that the trains travel when they are supposed to. Thus, we still must maintain control of the direction of traffic. If you recall, in both half-duplex and full-duplex environments, the station needed to know if the booth was in operation. The booth had to give the station a signal indicating that the bridge was present and that it was able to perform the control function. So we must still allow and check for this signal.

RS-232:   *Data set ready* (pin 6) must be present for data to be transmitted. When the private-line modem has power applied to it and the modem is functioning properly, DSR will be on. If the modem is not on, is in a test mode, or is faulty, DSR will not be high. Once the data terminal equipment checks for this signal and finds it on, it can be assured that the modem is available to perform its functions.

Assuming a half-duplex environment, the dispatcher at the depot makes sure that he turns on the engine headlights (RTS) when right-of-way of the facilities is desired. The far end can see the headlights (the *carrier*) and then knows that control of the track is being requested. Locally, the booth attendant gives a clear-to-send signal to the station. This interaction, as you can see, is the same as in the dial-up environment outlined in Chapter 3.

In a full-duplex environment, the signal interaction between the depots and booths is also the same as it was with the temporary bridge. Both stations keep the headlights turned on at all times because traffic can flow in both directions, simultaneously.

RS-232:   As you can see, ground, data, and most of the control leads of the communication facility are the same in either a private-line or dial-up environment. Regardless of whether you're in an HDX or FDX mode, the data and ground leads behave the same. Transmitted data is on pin 2, while received data is on pin 3. Pin 1 is protective ground, and signal ground is found on pin 7. The same interaction between RTS, CTS, and DCD occurs, dictated only by whether the facility is half-duplex or full-duplex. The main RS-232 difference is that pins 22 and 20 have no useful function in a private-line environment because the connection between

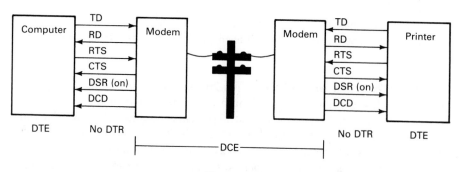

Figure 4-1

business machines is permanent. Also pin 6, data set ready, is on as long as the modem has power applied to it, whereas in a dial-up environment, it usually came on after the connection was established. The private line is represented in Figure 4-1.

Function	Pin	Lead Name (Abbr.)	Direction
Data	2	Transmitted data (TD)	From DTE
Data	3	Received data (RD)	From DCE
Control	4	Request to send (RTS)	From DTE
Control	5	Clear to send (CTS)	From DCE
Control	8	Data carrier detect (DCD)	From DCE
Control	6	Data set ready (DSR)	From DCE
Control	20	Data terminal ready (DTR)	Not used
Control	22	Ring indicator (RI)	Not used
Ground	1	Protective ground (PG)	N/A
Ground	7	Signal ground (SG)	N/A

Figure 4-2

REVIEW QUESTIONS

1. If the modem is off, what lead will not be high on the RS-232 interface?
2. In a private-line environment, how does the DTE know if the modem is not functioning?
3. DTR is used in a private-line environment to maintain the connection. True or false?
4. Because of different levels in a private line, signal ground behaves differently. True or false?
5. The RTS-CTS-DCD interactions are functionally the same in a private-line environment as they are on a dial-up line. True or false?
6. Complete the following chart.

Function	Pin	Lead Name (Abbr.)	Direction
Data	2	——	From DTE
Data	3	——	From DCE
Control	4	——	From DTE
Control	5	——	From DCE
Control	8	——	From DCE
Control	6	——	From DCE
Control	20	——	——
Control	22	——	——
Ground	1	——	N/A
Ground	7	——	N/A

5

Synchronous Environments

The trains up to now, consisting of boxcars and flatcars, have each had at least one engine and one caboose. The engine and caboose provided the timing of the traffic. At the destination station, once you saw an engine, you could bet that the rest of the train was following, right on time, with the caboose signaling the end of the train. Timing was on a train-by-train basis.

RS-232:   This transmission scheme, known as *asynchronous transmission*, has provided the basis for the bulk of our analogy up to this point. Because of start and stop bits, each character was individually *timed*, or *synchronized*. No special timing was needed. A different transmission scheme, known as *synchronous transmission*, will be introduced into the simile. But first, it is important to note a trend in the microcomputer field.

The use of personal computers (PCs) in synchronous environments is flourishing due to the communication software packages being written. De facto standards for terminals operating in synchronous private-line environments exist. Examples are IBM 3270 BSC/SDLC devices and controllers and IBM 2780/3780 BSC terminals.* These terminals and others operate in a synchronous environment, involving the timing aspect of the RS-232 interface. Because of the popularity of these terminal types, vast numbers of applications have been developed specifically for them. As the base of personal computers expands, the desire to access these existing applications also grows. In order for a personal computer to use these application packages, the PC must behave like a synchronous device. That means that if a PC wants to access applications normally intended for an IBM 3270 Binary Synchronous (BSC) device, the software in the PC must emulate all the device characteristics of the BSC terminal. This includes protocols, buffering, screen addressing, keyboard sequences, and other aspects. Software to emulate terminals is readily available for PCs. The specific characteristics of the terminal families are not as important to understanding RS-232 as the timing functions involved between the synchronous devices and their modems. Our scenario will describe the elements necessary for understanding timing in these terminals or emulating devices.

The need for longer and faster trains was discussed in Chapter 2. The basis for this need was that we had an engine and caboose for every seven or eight cars. This resulted in a lot of wasted track time. If you totaled the time on the track required for each engine and caboose, roughly 20 percent of the train was used for timing. Rather than send each train (character) out one at a time, with an engine and caboose, the Railroad Commission decided on a more economical and sophisticated method. The approach was temporarily to hold several small trains traveling to the same station and later ship them all at once as one long train.

*2780, 3270, and 3780 are trademarks of IBM Corp.

RS-232:   The communication term for this technique is *buffering*. Characters (trains) are *buffered* at the originating station (business machine) into logical groupings for transmission as a single group. The need for an engine and caboose still exists, but in a different manner, as we shall see in a moment.

Once a method of buffering trains at one location was discovered, several benefits were realized. Money was saved due to the fact that fewer engines and cabooses were needed. Also, more time was available for actual train traffic because of the reduced need for engines and cabooses.

However, a couple of factors must be dealt with in this environment. The longer a train is, the greater the possibility for it to jump the track, causing garbling and derailment of the boxcars and flatcars. The major cause of derailment is either the track or the speed at which the train was traveling. The quality of the track is a major factor influencing the smoothness of train operation. The higher the quality, the less likelihood of derailment. A lower-quality track may collapse, causing a bit of a mess (or, I should say, a mess of bits). The tracks have already been designed by the engineers and established by the installers. So, we must assume that the tracks were built and conditioned for such a traffic load.

However, no one has addressed the actual rate of speed. How fast should a train be allowed to travel and who controls this speed limit over the bridge?

RS-232:   The control of this speed limit is dubbed *timing*. Instead of individually synchronizing each character, the larger group of buffered data is synchronized by means of the timing element. In contrast with asynchronous transmission, this method is known as *synchronous transmission*. The engine and caboose are still present, indicating the beginning and end of the train. However, they assume a different meaning. In asynchronous transmission, the two units were start and stop bits, providing the timing for the individual characters. In a synchronous environment, the engine and caboose represent characters by themselves, indicating the start of a *block* of text and the end of that unit of text. They are not used for the function of timing but for the framing of a block of text. Timing is handled in a totally different fashion in synchronous transmission.

So, how will timing of trains be handled when our trains are longer and faster? First of all, the speed limit for the tracks should be established. How fast can trains successfully travel across the permanent or temporary bridge? The speed limit should be fast enough to allow the maximum number of trains to cross the bridge, yet slow enough to allow the trains to reach their destination safely.

The type and size of tracks used, for the most part, dictate the speed limit to be enforced. Based on the bridge engineers' specifications for the railroad lines, a rate will be established. Once established, enforcement of this limit is all that remains for a smooth flow of high-speed trains.

RS-232:   The speed limit is usually expressed in *bits per second (bps)*. This rate is the number of 1s and 0s that can be transmitted in the period of one second. Once the speed is known, you can divide it by the number of bits per character to determine how many characters can be transmitted in a second. Typical synchronous speeds are 1200, 2400, 4800, 9600, and 19,200 bps. If the speed of a communication facility is 2400 bps and the length of each character is 8 bits, approximately 300 characters can be transmitted over the line each second. The RS-232 standard allows for speeds up to 20,000 bps. Speeds near the maximum are common in a private-line environment. In a dial-up environment, synchronous speeds of 4800 bps are more typical. However, technology is advancing to the point where speeds approaching the maximum rate allowed by the standard can be attained over dial-up lines.

Having established a speed limit for the rails, somehow we must provide for the regulation or control of the limit over the bridge. Thus, trains need some mechanism for controlling how fast they should proceed down the railroad lines.

RS-232:   Timing must be provided to control the rate at which data are transmitted and received on the lines.

The speed of the trains can be controlled at a number of different points in our bridge connection. Analyzing the various elements in our analogy, an obvious choice is the train station, because one exists at each end of the bridge. The depot at the origination site could regulate the speed of all outgoing trains. Outbound trains would be informed by the station of the correct speed at which to travel. At the same depot, the speed of the inbound trains could be monitored. The depot operator could then determine if the train is traveling at the correct speed (Figure 5-1).

RS-232:   The speed control of the outbound traffic is termed *transmit timing*. Transmit timing is the clocking rate of the data transmission. The characters are "clocked" out onto the line at whatever rate the transmit timing lead is providing. When transmit timing is provided by the train depot (DTE), it is supplied on pin 24. Some business machines have an option of either *internal* or *external timing*. When the DTE is to be the source for the timing, internal timing should be selected. In this case, timing is provided by the computer, terminal, or printer on pin 24 for data tranmission.

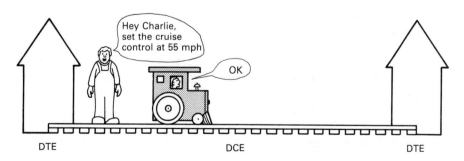

DTE   DCE   DTE

Figure 5-1

Figure 5-2

Another potential location for train speed regulation is the booths. The booths could provide the depot with the speed at which the trains should depart from the depot and cross the bridge. Because the booths are directly connected to the bridge, they are in a better position to know the quality of the facility. Because of this, speed control by the booths is the more common of the two possibilities (Figure 5-2).

RS-232:   The term for this is also *transmit timing*. However, this type of timing provided by the booth (modem) is considered to be a DCE source. A different lead, pin 15, is used to indicate transmit timing from a DCE source. In this case, if we looked at the business machine (DTE), the option for timing would be set for external timing. But from the DCE (modem) point of view, the modem would be optioned for internal timing. It is important to note that this could be a confusing option unless one considers the "source" of the timing. In summary, if the DTE is to provide the transmit timing, this timing will be provided on pin 24; if the DCE will provide it, the timing will be provided on pin 15 (Figure A-1). Thus, we have an option as to who is going to provide the speed limit (*clock rate*) of the data transfer.

At the booth across the bridge, the speed of the train could be monitored for an indication of the speed limit. Why is this required? The receiving depot must know the speed at which the trains will be arriving. This is necessary to allow the receiving station to check the train cars it received to ensure the accuracy of the shipment. To allow for this, we will let the booth derive the speed of the train as it passes by. Then, the booth operator will pass the derived speed limit to the depot for proper reception of the train. When these two components, booth and depot, are working in sync, the trains can be properly received and analyzed (Figure 5-3).

Figure 5-3

RS-232: This is known as *receiver signal element timing* (DCE source). For ease of reference, we will call it *receive timing*. This timing is found on pin 17. Typically, the modem can generate its own receive timing. However, it is often more efficient to derive the receive timing from the data being received. If the modem can extract the speed limit from the data received, this timing can be passed on pin 17 to the business machine, which uses this clock rate to receive the data properly.

At this end, we also have to allow for the transmit timing function. The fewer sources for timing that are used, the less of a chance for timing problems to occur. To minimize the number of sources for timing, the following connection is possible. If the derived timing on pin 17 is looped up to pin 15 (transmit timing), *synchronization* is usually more easily maintained, because it comes from a single source. We have also satisfied the transmit timing requirement at this end by using the receive timing (Figure 5-4). As you can see, there is a single source for the timing. By looping the receive timing at one end to the transmit timing lead, there is less timing to keep in sync. Often, in modems, this option is known as *slave timing* — the transmit timing (pin 15) at one end is *slaved* (derived) from the receive timing lead (pin 17).

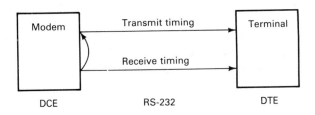

Figure 5-4

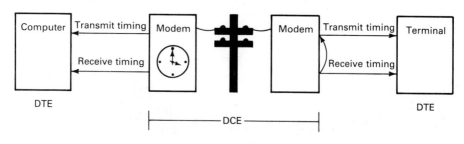

Figure 5-5

If you follow the timing all the way through the network, you can see that a single source can be used to provide both transmit and receive timing at both ends of the facility. This is the ideal environment to set up for synchronous transmission (Figure 5-5).

As we have seen, the key difference between asynchronous and synchronous transmission is the aspect of timing. Asynchronous transmission requires timing on a character basis. A typical example of this is a Teletype* terminal. Each character is surrounded by start and stop bits for the purpose of timing. In most data communications over telephone lines requiring speeds greater than 1200 bps, the synchronous mode of operation will be used. With synchronous transmission, a timing signal is provided by either the DTE or DCE for synchronization of the data transmission. Special leads on the RS-232 interface have been set aside for this timing, as shown in Figure 5-6.

Function	Pin	Lead name	Source
Timing	15	Transmit timing	From DCE
Timing	17	Receive timing	From DCE
Timing	24	Transmit timing	From DTE

Figure 5-6

As a final review note, the more engineers trying to pilot the train, the more possibilities for traffic problems. In a communication environment, the more sources providing the timing, the greater the chances for mismatched clock rates. To limit the potential for errors, use the fewest number of timing sources by deriving the timing (slave timing) from a single source whenever possible.

*Teletype is a trademark of Teletype Corp.

REVIEW QUESTIONS

1. A transmission scheme in which characters are individually timed is _____.

2. A transmission scheme in which characters are temporarily stored until a block can be sent out at a predetermined clock rate is _____.

3. Temporarily storing characters for later transmission is known as _____.

4. The aspect that distinguishes asynchronous transmission from synchronous transmission is the _____ element.

5. Transmission rates are generally expressed in _____.

6. The RS-232 standard allows a maximum speed of _____ bps.

7. There are two major types of timing in an RS-232 environment, _____ and _____ timing.

8. If the DTE is providing the transmit timing, it is found on pin _____. If the modem is providing the transmit timing, it is found on pin _____.

9. The receive timing is found on pin _____.

10. The modem option that loops pin 17 to pin 15 is known as _____ timing.

11. Explain the differences between internal and external timing as it relates to RS-232 signals.

12. Explain slave timing and why it is used.

13. Compare asynchronous transmission and synchronous transmission.

14. Complete the following timing chart.

Function	Pin	Lead Name (Abbr.)	Source
Timing	15	_____	_____
Timing	17	_____	_____
Timing	_____	Transmit timing	From DTE

6

Secondary Signals and Flow Control

We have been discussing the bridge across the body of water. In these discussions we have implied that only trains can cross the bridge over the tracks. We will now identify other vehicles that may cross the water to maximize the use of the bridge.

As long as we are using the bridge to provide rail service across the water, why not expand the offering to allow smaller objects to cross? For example, the way the bridges are constructed, some unused space exists along the sides of the tracks. Let us optimize the use of the facilities by using the remaining space beside the tracks as a sidewalk for slower-moving traffic such as pedestrians, bicycles, and so on. This narrow strip is a very thin band of concrete or steel. The band width is so narrow that people or bicycles can normally go in only one direction at a time. Have you heard this before? This was the characteristic of HDX. Refer to Figure 6-1 for representation of the extra space along the sides of the bridge.

In our earlier discussions, we outlined the procedure for control of HDX facilities like this. The same concept of requesting to send by the station and getting a clear-to-send signal for crossing is applicable, as is the indication to the other side that a depot is requesting to send something across. However, because of the limited side-band width, these signals are considered secondary and are reserved only for smaller traffic, not the large trains that run on the tracks. Even though the side bands permit only limited traffic, they serve a very useful purpose, as we shall see.

RS-232: Pins of this nature carry secondary signals. They function in the same manner as their primary counterparts but control secondary channels of the communication facility (Figure A-1). For example, RTS becomes *secondary request to send*. The same *secondary* nomenclature applies to *clear to send* and *data carrier detect*. In addition, there are *secondary transmitted* and *received data* channels. Intelligent modems, capable of transmitting diagnostic information, use these secondary data channels for testing and trouble-reporting purposes. However, unless intelligent devices are being used, these secondry data channels are rarely utilized. Nevertheless, *secondary data carrier detect,* also known as *secondary receive*

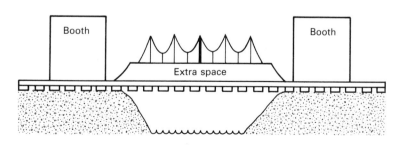

Figure 6-1

Function	Pin	Name	Direction
Data	14	Secondary transmitted data	From DTE
Data	16	Secondary received data	From DCE
Control	19	Secondary request to send	From DTE
Control	13	Secondary clear to send	From DCE
Control	12	Secondary carrier detect	From DCE

Figure 6-2

line signal detector, plays an important role in the area of transmission control. See Figure 6-2 for a listing of the *secondary leads* on the RS-232 interface.

In half-duplex environments, these secondary signals have a key role. As you recall, when a half-duplex facility is being utilized, primary data and control signals are used in one direction at a time. Information is transmitted in a single direction with great success under normal circumstances. But what if a problem occurs at one end of the facility? What type of problems could occur? The next few paragraphs define the types of potential problems and describe their solutions using these secondary signals. We will temporarily ignore our analogy and utilize pure RS-232 terminology for the remainder of this chapter.

Let's focus on a specific configuration of a computer transmitting payroll information across the communication facility to a receive-only printer over a half-duplex facility. There is no need to cover how the connection is established between the two devices, as we have been through that sequence in earlier chapters. So let's assume that the connection is established, either dial-up or private line, and the proper signals have been exchanged to allow the computer to transmit data to the printer as shown in Figure 6-3.

Things are going smoothly until, after minutes or hours of data traffic, the supply of paper being fed through the printer begins to get a little low. As the printer continues to chug along, the last sheet of paper rolls through the printer. The problem should now be intuitively obvious to the most casual observer. The computer will continue to throw data at the printer. The printer, however, receives the data but can't transcribe the bits onto the paper. Remember we are out of the pulp. So the

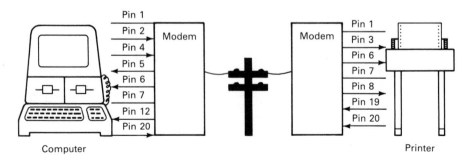

Figure 6-3

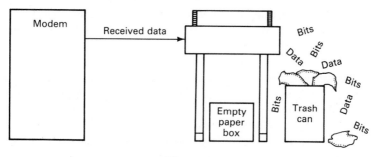

Figure 6-4

data are either printed on the bare printer platen or are lost (Figure 6-4). This could be catastrophic, especially if the next item to be printed would have been your paycheck! Let's solve the problem so we won't shortchange ourselves in the future.

In a half-duplex environment, the primary data path is available in only one direction at a time. However, the secondary data and control signals are available to be used from either the computer or printer end. We'll utilize these secondary signals to control the loss of data and keep the "cards and letters" and checks coming.

The best way to prevent the loss of the received data is to provide a means of notifying the computer, or transmitting end, of the problem. In this case we have what is known as a "paper out" condition. If the computer is aware of a problem at the far-end printer, it can temporarily halt data transmission until the problem is cleared. Once a new batch of paper is threaded through the printer, the printer will be ready to crank out your check. The printing can resume after the printer gives an indication to the computer that all is O.K.

Peripheral manufacturers capitalized on the availability of secondary control signals on the RS-232 interface to prevent the catastrophe. The solution was to have the printer, or receiving device, always give a positive indication when data could be received. This was made possible by having the printer keep its secondary request to send (SRTS) lead high. Because these secondary signals behave the same as our primary ones, this caused secondary carrier to be transmitted back to the computer. The computer was constantly monitoring its secondary data carrier detect (SDCD) lead, pin 12. As long as pin 12 was high on the interface, data could be transmitted.

Should a paper-out or other problem condition occur, the printer would drop its SRTS lead, causing no secondary carrier to be evident at the computer end. If SDCD was low, the computer would cease transmission because of the indication that a problem existed at the far end. Once the problem was cleared, its SDCD/ SRLSD pin would come back on because the printer at the far end would once again raise its SRTS signal.The computer could now successfully print your paycheck.

RS-232:   Even though we are in a half-duplex environment, we can still pass these secondary signals in the opposite direction of the primary signals. This is possible because we are using a secondary channel of the communication facility that is separate from the primary channel. The technical term for this operation is *reverse channel*. *Reverse channel* is used for the specific function of supervisory control.

Another frequent use of reverse channel is to prevent buffer overflow. If a device is receiving data, the bits can be placed in the device's buffer for printing at whatever speed the printer is capable of. Depending on the size, the device's buffer may fill up to the point that it overflows, or loses data. Reverse channel can be applied in the same manner as in our paper-out condition to prevent buffer overflow and, consequently, loss of data.

Half-duplex flow control utilizing the secondary channels, in addition to being termed *reverse channel,* performs what is known as a *hardware XON/XOFF* function. To understand the meaning of this function, we must revert to a full-duplex environment.

With FDX, some devices, such as printers, can monitor their buffer or paper supply electronically. If either the paper is getting low or the buffer is reaching its capacity, the printer can transmit a *device control character*. This character is transmitted over the primary-data channel to the computer, indicating that data transmission should be temporarily suspended. The printer then notifies the computer when transmission can resume by transmitting a different device control character. Full-duplex allows for this two-way communication to occur. This is often termed a *software XON/XOFF* function. A physical character is transmitted.

In a half-duplex environment, data can be transmitted in only one direction at a time, limiting the printer's ability to transmit a device control character. The RS-232 secondary signals, reverse channel, are used to accomplish the XON/XOFF function. This is termed *hardware XON/XOFF,* because it is handled by the RS-232 interface.

Reverse channel can be used for other purposes in a communication environment, but the preceding examples demonstrate two of the major uses of these secondary control signals.

REVIEW QUESTIONS

1. The main channel of a communication facility is the _____ channel.
2. _____ signals can be used to solve printer control problems. Explain another method of flow control.
3. List the two secondary data signals.
4. List the three secondary control signals.
5. The term for using secondary RTS for supervisory control is _____.
6. Explain the printer or buffer overflow problem and how to solve it.

CHAPTER

7

Cross
Connections

Only one more area of discussion is necessary to give you a full understanding of the RS-232 interface, that of *cross connections* between devices when no communication facilities will be used. Cross connections, perhaps the most important item to a microcomputer user, are generally the least understood. How do you connect a serial device, such as a printer, to the serial interface on your computer? By the end of this chapter, this cross connection will seem as easy as powering up your system.

The bridge scenario, thus far, has provided an excellent foundation for a thorough description of a data communication environment. The train depots and booths stood for DTE and DCE, respectively. Between the two booths was the bridge, which represented the telephone lines for communication facilities. Recall that the bridge could be of a permanent or temporary nature, allowing for the distinction between private and dial-up lines.

We have reached the point when the bridge is no longer needed—the big river is now just a trickle of water.

RS-232: DCE is no longer going to be present. Specifically, the modems and telephone lines are not needed to connect two business machines if they are sitting side by side, or at least within 50 feet of each other. Due to electrical capacities, the RS-232 standard limits the cabling distance to 50 feet. Keep this in mind when locally connecting two devices with serial interfaces.

Even though the big river of water is gone, the trickling creek has to be accommodated for. For purposes of discussion we will design a shortcut under the water—a tunnel. This tunnel must have the capability to handle the trains as if they were crossing a bridge. So, the same ''handshaking'' must occur for the depots to operate as normal stations would, even though we're in a different environment. The tunnel must be built in such a fashion that the depots don't have to change their procedures for train traffic. In short, the tunnel must emulate the booths and the bridge. This is a requirement to allow the standard stations to be built to operate on either a bridge or tunnel type of facility.

RS-232: Business machines are manufactured with *serial* interfaces that normally conform to the RS-232-C standard. If the standard is adhered to, RS-232 leads (pins) should be similar for any DTE. This also implies that these business machines are set up to expect the standard RS-232 signals normally provided by the DCE. Specifically, a modem would supply the proper signals to allow the DTE to function properly during its data transmission. When a port is configured to expect the signals normally provided by a modem, that port is said to be *emulating* data terminal equipment. While it is expecting to receive these signals, it also will generate signals such as request to send and data terminal ready, which are output signals from DTE. If, on the other hand, the port is emulating data communication equipment, leads such as data set ready, clear to send, and data carrier detect are output signals generated from the port. When either of these categories, DTE or DCE, is being emulated, the proper output signals should be generated and the corresponding input signals can be expected. Recall from earlier chapters that these standard signals fell into four categories, ground, data, control, and timing. When connecting these leads to allow local connections between machines (without modems), all four categories of leads on the RS-232-C interface must be crossed to emulate a communication environment as if modems and lines were present. Because the cross-connections cable is used when no modems are present, we generally refer to it as a *null-modem cable*. The following discussion describes the cross connections required to build this type of cable.

We have already outlined the basic need for the tunnel to be built, emulating the booths and the bridge. The easiest way to accomplish this is to divide the requirements of the stations into four categories: ground, train tracks, traffic control, and speed limit. We will always view these categories from the stations' perspectives. The reason for this is that we are currently dealing with only the two depots (Figure 7-1).

RS-232:   The first and easiest category is *ground*. Because these signals are present for protection and signal reference, merely allow for them in the null-modem cable. *Protective ground* (pin 1) is electrically bonded to the machine or equipment frame, while *signal ground* (pin 7) establishes the common reference for all other interchange circuits except pin 1. So, in a null-modem cable, merely provide these two pins straight through from DTE to DTE. No crossovers are required (Figure 7-2).

The second part of the tunnel emulates the tracks used for the departure and arrival of trains. Again, we view these tracks from the stations' perspectives. Trains departing from station A arrive at station B on a track set aside for receiving trains. The converse is also true. The tunnel should allow for a crossover of these tracks to

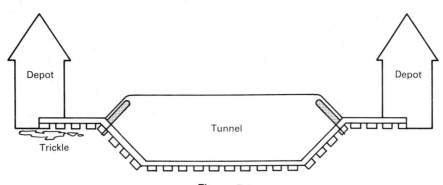

Figure 7-1

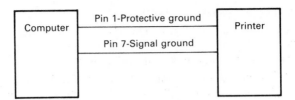

Figure 7-2

prevent head-on collisions of trains. This crossover allows for proper departure and arrival of trains at each station through the tunnel.

RS-232: This category includes the *data* leads (pins 2 and 3). Pin 2 is used for transmitted data, and pin 3 for received data. Both are normally present at both ends. The exception might be pin 2 at the printer end. Why? You guessed it: Printers do not usually transmit data; they receive only. Data are transmitted over pin 2 from one machine and received on pin 3 at the other. To allow for proper data transmission and reception at both machines, cross pin 2 at one end with pin 3 of the other end. Repeat this at both ends as represented in Figure 7-3.

So far we have accommodated both ground and data leads in the interface—50 percent of our null-modem connection. All that remain are the control and timing leads.

Traffic control was one of the major problems that had to be overcome for proper use of the bridge facilities. Control was used to regulate the flow of trains. The regulation involved both when the bridge would remain lowered for crossing and when a train could actually cross it. We must approach our tunnel connection with the same regulatory concerns, even though a bridge isn't used.

RS-232: We must allow for actual DTE leads as well as emulated DCE leads in the cross-connection cable. Data terminal equipment (DTE)– provided signals are all that are present in a null-modem cable. This limitation forces us to provide DCE signals with available DTE signals. Specifically, the DTE signals (RTS and DTR) must be used to provide or emulate the DCE-provided signals (DSR, CTS, and DCD) that would have existed in a normal telecommunication environment.

If you consider the configuration, two DTEs are to be locally connected with merely a cable between them. These business machines, built for a communication environment, are expecting the standard RS-232 control signals usually received

Function	Pin	Pin	Function
Transmitted data	2	2	Transmitted data
Received data	3	3	Received data

Figure 7-3

through the modem. We will now explain how the DCE signals can be emulated by the available DTE-provided signals, RTS and DTR.

We must design the aspect of the tunnel that normally would control the indications and maintenance of the bridge across the water. Because we have no booths to control the bridge and give any indications of status, we use the signal system that is provided by the depot. If the depot is manned to receive trains, an indication is normally given to the booth. This signal lets the booth know that the bridge connection should be maintained and trains could be received.

The depots, even in our tunnel, are still expecting signals indicating that trains have tracks available to them. With no booths available, we have to allow somehow for these signals. To do so, we use the depot's signal at one end of the tunnel to emulate the absent signal at the other end. We duplicate this emulation at the other end of the tunnel. This technique allows depot A to receive the required indication of a connection, even without the presence of a booth.

RS-232:   DTR (pin 20) is ordinarily provided by the DTE (depot) to indicate that power is on at the terminal and is also used to maintain the connection in a dial-up environment. For an indication that the line is established between DTEs, the DCE normally gives a signal on pin 6 (DSR). As long as DSR is on, one can assume that the DCE, both modem and line, is available for data transmission. If pin 6 is not present, the line or connection is not available. To emulate DSR at both ends, we strap the DTR signal at one device across to pin 6 at the other device. The same strapping is done in the other direction. By strapping pin 20 across to pin 6, whenever DTR is high (the machine power is on), the other end will get an indication that the transmission line is available. If power is off, the other end will not have DSR, indicating that the communication path is not established. The pins should be crossed as shown in Figure 7-4.

RS-232:   The other element of the control function on the interface is *path control*. Three leads were necessary for this function (Figure 7-5). RTS was the headlight on the train, turned on by the depot. This light was seen at the far end on pin 8, data carrier detect. CTS was the indication from the booth that a depot had control of the tracks and could send trains across the bridge. When only a single track was available on the bridge (half-duplex), path control was extremely important; when two-way traffic was allowed simultaneously (full-duplex), this concern was somewhat relaxed, but the signals were still present.

In a tunnel, the same track-control signals must be allowed for. The booth

Function	Pin	Pin	Function
Data set ready	6	6	Data set ready
Data terminal ready	20	20	Data terminal ready

Figure 7-4

Function		Pin
Request to send	RTS	4
Clear to send	CTS	5
Data carrier detect	DCD	8

Figure 7-5

signals are not present. We must provide these by utilizing available signals from the depot's point of view. Of the three signals necessary for train path control, only one is available at each end. This signal is the headlight indication of a request to send a train to the other depot. How are we going to get three signals from only one? Believe it or not, this can be accomplished rather easily.

Consider the source of each signal. The request to send a train is from the depot. The other two are normally from the two separate booths. The signal indicating that is it clear to send the trains is normally given by the local booth back to the originating depot, whereas the other depot receives its indication of a possible train arrival locally from its booth. Of course, the only time that this signal is given is if the request-to-send signal is raised at the other end by the originating depot.

To allow for this same interaction with neither booths nor bridge, we must once again emulate some signals. The request-to-send and clear-to-send signals occur at the same end of the tunnel. Thus, we can accomplish the RTS-CTS interaction by faking out the depot so that whenever the headlight is turned on, the depot can see it reflected as if it were seeing the signal normally provided by the booth. By placing a mirror or reflector at the entrance to the tunnel, whenever the headlight is on, the depot will see a signal and think it is getting a clear-to-send signal. In this way, at the originating depot, the path-control requirements are met. The far-end depot can still see the headlight through the tunnel and still receives the signals it expects for reception of train traffic.

RS-232: Technically, we will apply the same concept of mirroring the RTS signal back to the originating machine. RTS (pin 4) is normally generated by the DTE. For data transmission to be allowed, CTS (pin 5) must be received by the same DTE. So, we loop the RTS signal back to the originating DTE by wiring it back to pin 5 (CTS). Pictorially, this is represented as in Figure 7-6.

Whenever the DTE—for example, a computer—raises RTS, it immediately receives a CTS signal indicating that data transmission is now possible. As for the need of the receiving device to have an indication that data will be arriving, we must provide for DCD (pin 8) to be derived from the same source, RTS. Thus, we also connect RTS (pin 4) at the originating DTE to the data carrier detect lead, pin 8, at the far end, as shown in Figure 7-7.

Function	Pin
Request to send	4
Clear to send	5

Figure 7-6

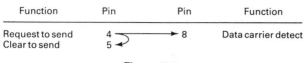

Figure 7-7

By making these cross connections, not only will a CTS signal be given, but when RTS is raised, the other end will also receive its DCD signal, indicating that data transmission is possible. Repeat these connections at both DTEs to allow two-way transmission. Whether the terminals are set up for HDX or FDX, path-control requirements have been met in the null-modem cable.

RS-232: *Timing* leads remain. You will recall that the only situation in which timing leads were required was in a synchronous environment. If the null-modem cable is being built for an asynchronous terminal interconnection, you can ignore this next section and proceed to the discussion on secondary signals. For a synchronous environment, read on.

As booths and bridges were being designed to allow faster trains across them, speed limits were established for smooth train traffic. When possible, a single speed limit was used to regulate trains in both directions, typically controlled by the booth. We are without booths in our tunnel to provide this function. So, we must either provide a traffic cop for this or leave this function up to the depots.

Some depots have the capability to regulate the speed of the traffic, while others do not. If the depots can control the speed limit, let them. Simply decide which depot will regulate the speed, and let the other depot use the same regulation for its train traffic through the tunnel.

In an environment in which neither depot can regulate the speed limit of the train, hire a traffic cop. This patrolman, positioned in the middle of the tunnel, provides speed control in both directions. High-speed train traffic can be regulated without the risk of derailment with the help of this traffic cop.

RS-232:   The two situations just described relate to synchronous environments in which either the DTE can provide timing or an external source of timing is required. In the case of the latter, a null-modem cable cannot be built to satisfy the timing need. In a normal telecommunication environment of this nature, timing must be provided by the DCE or modem. Because there is no DCE when locally connecting two devices, a separate unit must be placed between the devices. This unit is often termed a *synchronous null-modem device* or *synchronous modem eliminator*. It eliminates the modems as the standard null-modem cable does, yet allows for timing. Not only are the ground, data, and control leads taken care of, as previously described, but timing is also provided by the box (Figure 7-8).

What if at least one of the DTEs can provide the timing? We go back to the null-modem cable. There is need for only a single source of timing. If both DTEs have this capability, decide which one will be optioned to provide it. Once op-

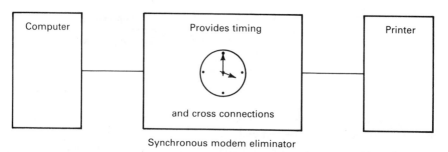

Synchronous modem eliminator

Figure 7-8

tioned, the timing will be provided by the terminal on pin 24, transmit signal element timing (DTE source). This is the timing that will be used for both devices, whether transmitting or receiving. Satisfying the need for timing at both ends is rather simple. Because a single source of timing is required, merely connect all of the associated timing leads together, both transmit and receive. Connect pin 24 to pins 17 and 15 at one end, and connect one of these leads across to pins 15 and 17 tied together at the other end. The fashion in which pins 15 and 17 are connected really doesn't matter as long as both sides are eventually connected to the timing source on pin 24. This is depicted in Figure 7-9.

Now that all timing leads are connected, synchronous transmission can successfully occur. In fact, pin 15 on the DTE side that provides the timing doesn't need to be connected at all. The source DTE is providing its own transmit timing; it will ignore whatever timing is presented to it on pin 15. We have built a synchronous null-modem cable, whereby one of the DTEs is providing the timing.

Figure 7-10 summarizes an asynchronous null-modem cable. To work in a synchronous environment with the DTE providing the timing, add the lead connections shown in Figure 7-11.

In either an asynchronous or synchronous environment, with our null-modem cables, we should still be "on track with RS-232."

RS-232: One final aspect of a null-modem cable is *printer control.* In Chapter 6, we covered the need for a printer to notify the computer at the distant end of an alarm condition. Specifically, the secondary control signal (reverse channel) was used to indicate that a paper-out condition had occurred. When modems are not used, as in the local attachment of a printer to a computer's serial port, the same

Function	Pin	Pin	Function
Transmit timing	15	15	Transmit timing
Receive timing	17	17	Receive timing
External timing	24		

Figure 7-9

Category	Function	Pin	Pin	Function
Ground	PG	1 ——————— 1		PG
Ground	SG	7 ——————— 7		SG
Data	TD	2	2	TD
Data	RD	3	3	RD
Control	RTS	4	4	RTS
Control	CTS	5	5	CTS
Control	DCD/RLSD	8	8	DCD/RLSD
Control	DSR	6	6	DSR
Control	DTR	20	20	DTR

Figure 7-10

Category	Function	Pin	Pin	Function
Timing	RT	17	15	TT
Timing	EXT-TT	24	17	RT

Figure 7-11

concept is often applied. So, in addition to the standard null-modem cable, cross connections for printer control may be required.

To cross-connect properly between the computer and the printer, the technical specification for the serial ports must be reviewed. First, determine which lead is held high by the printer to indicate that the printer is functioning properly—no paper-out condition. Usually this lead is secondary request to send (pin 19), but often on a printer, pin 20 (DTR) provides this function. Whichever is used, this lead will still function in the same manner. However, the lead must be cross-connected to a lead at the computer end that is required before the computer can transmit.

At the computer end, a lead must be found that is important enough so that the computer can transmit data if it is on. If it is not on, it must prohibit the computer from transmitting data. Secondary data carrier detect is sometimes used for this function. But this signal is not always present on serial interfaces. Data set ready (pin 6) is a lead that is usually monitored by the computer for regulating when data can be transmitted. When modems are used in a dial-up environment, this lead indicates that a line is available for transmission. If this lead (pin 6) is required before the computer can transmit, merely connect it to the lead at the printer end used for printer control. Once connected, the computer and printer behave in a normal fashion, as if there were modems between the devices. Figure 7-12 illustrates this connection. Do not cross-connect pin 20 to pin 6 as previously described. If you did, pin 6 would never fluctuate, defeating the purpose of the cross connection for flow control. Although these two leads may vary, depending on the devices, the same principle for printer control is applied as in a null-modem cable.

There are many ways of building the null-modem cable. Figure 7-13 outlines other possibilities.

Function	Pin	Pin	Function
Secondary RTS	19 ⟶ 6		Data set ready

Figure 7-12

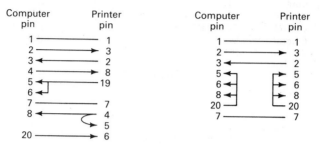

Figure 7-13

The particular null-modem cable used depends on the signals required and provided by the data terminal equipment and is affected by flow-control leads. Consult Appendixes F and G for further possible cross-connections.

REVIEW QUESTIONS

1. The cable that can be built for the local attachment of a printer to a computer's modem port is generally called a _____.

2. _____ connections are used to emulate the leads normally provided by a modem.

3. If the DTE cannot provide the timing, a separate device can be purchased to provide both timing and all other cross connections. This device is a _____.

4. The distance limitation outlined by the RS-232-C standard is _____ feet.

5. Name the four categories of leads.

6. All signals used in an asynchronous null-modem cable must be emulated or provided by the _____.

7. The two ground leads, normally wired straight through in a null-modem cable, are found on pins _____ and _____.

8. Transmitted data, pin 2, at one end should be crossed over to pin _____ at the receiving end in a null-modem cable.

9. RTS, pin 4, should be looped back, locally, to provide _____, on pin _____, and then across to pin _____ to provide data carrier detect.

10. DTR, pin _____, can be used to provide _____ (pin 6) at the opposite end.

11. The _____ signal normally indicates that a modem was available for use and generally controlled the computer's transmission.

12. If the DTE is providing the timing, it is found on pin _____.

13. In the case of question 12, which three leads should be wired together?

14. Which category of leads differentiates a synchronous null-modem cable from an asynchronous null-modem cable?

15. _____, pin 19, is usually used for printer control and must be crossed to a lead such as data set ready or clear to send at the computer end.

16. Explain, conceptually, how pin 19, secondary request to send, could potentially be used for flow control in a normal communication environment. Assume that the computer at the far end does not monitor any of its secondary signals. (Hint: Use RTS at the printer end and data carrier detect and data set ready at the far end.)

17. What is the "golden rule" when dealing with straight-through RD-232 cables or null-modem cables?

8

Interfacing

Equipment

The application of the RS-232 interface is widespread in mainframes, minicomputers, microcomputers, printers, and all types of terminals. The basic principles of the standard are implemented in such devices; however, minor variations may occur from device to device. These variations become extremely significant when interfacing different combinations of computers, printers, and terminals. Consequently, several aspects of the specific interfaces, which must be reviewed prior to a successful interconnection, will now be pursued.

Installations of devices to be locally connected may generally be implemented using the previously discussed null-modem cable. This is typically the case when both devices are configured as data terminal equipment (DTE). Recall that such devices generally provide the signals listed in Figure 8-1. The directions of these signals are important as they are output from the DTE. We say that the device is *emulating DTE* in that it generates the signals normally provided by DTE. Also, it is expecting to receive the signals normally generated by data communication equipment (DCE), such as a modem. So, in a null-modem cable, the output signals from the DTE were cross-connected to input signals such as those listed in Figure 8-2.

RS-232: A general rule may be established as follows: When cross-connecting between devices, make sure that an output signal goes to an input signal, and vice versa. A quick review of our null-modem cable shows that transmitted data (output) is cross-connected to received data (input). Also, data terminal ready (output) is connected to data set ready (input). Whether dealing with a null-modem ca-

Pin	Function	Direction
2	Transmitted data	From DTE
4	Request to send	From DTE
11	Reverse channel (SRTS)	From DTE
19	Reverse channel (SRTS)	From DTE
20	Data terminal ready	From DTE

Figure 8-1

Pin	Function	Direction
3	Received data	To DTE
5	Clear to send	To DTE
6	Data set ready	To DTE
8	Data carrier detect	To DTE
12	Secondary DCD	To DTE

Figure 8-2

| IBM PC | | | Model 16 |
Direction	Pin	Pin	Direction
N/A	1 ——————— 1		N/A
From PC	2	2	From Model 16
To PC	3	3	To Model 16
From PC	4	4	From Model 16
To PC	5	5	To Model 16
To PC	6	6	Not used
N/A	7	7	N/A
To PC	8	8	To Model 16
From PC	20	20	From Model 16

Figure 8-3

ble or any cable for cross connection, the general rule holds true.

For example, when connecting an IBM PC,* using the serial port provided by the asynchronous communications adapter, to a Radio Shack Model 16† computer, a standard null-modem cable will work. This is because both of these machines are configured for connection to a modem (DCE). In other words, they are emulating DTE. This interconnection might be required to allow for a transfer of data files or programs between machines. The cable would connect the pins on the RS-232 interfaces as shown in Figure 8-3. Note that the general rule applies. Output signals are connected to input signals. Specifically, transmitted data (output) on the IBM port is connected to received data (input) on the Model 16 port. The same applies to the RTS-CTS-DCD pins as well as the DTR-DSR pin assignments. Ease of implementation can be maintained if the rule is followed.

If the port is configured to emulate DTE, as in the example in Figure 8-3, a modem can be attached to the device with a straight-through cable. From the chart of both computers, one can see the signals that are normally expected by the modem. They are generally ground leads, transmit data, request to send, and data terminal ready. Thus, when connecting a computer, terminal, or printer to a modem, these signals must generally be provided.

What is the significance of a port that, conversely, emulates data communication equipment? The implication is that the device is providing signals normally provided by a modem. These signals are outlined in Figure 8-2. When connecting a standard terminal or printer to a port emulating DCE, the likelihood of cross connections is reduced. By applying our general rule, you can visualize that transmitted data, which is output from the terminal on pin 2, is already input to the port that is emulating DCE. Also, received data is provided by the DCE port as input to the terminal on pin 3. The crossing of a few leads may be required for an item such as flow control, but for the most part, a cable with straight-through leads may be used

*IBM PC is a trademark of International Business Machines.
†Model 16 is a trademark of Radio Shack.

Direction	Pin	Pin	Direction
N/A	1 ———— 1		N/A
To Apple	2 ———— 2		From 43
From Apple	3 ———— 3		To 43
To Apple	4 ———— 4		From 43
From Apple	5 ———— 5		To 43
From Apple	6 ———— 6		To 43
N/A	7 ———— 7		N/A
From Apple	8 ———— 8		To 43
To Apple	20 ———— 20		From 43

Figure 8-4

as depicted Figure 8-4. In this particular instance, a Teletype Model 43* teleprinter is being connected to an Apple II Plus† computer with a Super Serial Card.‡ The Super Serial Card is configured in the terminal position. Note that our rule still applies even though a straight-through cable is being used.

From the preceding examples you can surmise that one of the first factors to consider when interfacing equipment using RS-232 ports is whether a port or terminal is configured to emulate DTE- or DCE-provided signals. The best way to determine this is to review the device documentation. Consult the user's manual for this information. Ordinarily, the manuals that are provided with the equipment contain the information necessary to determine the direction and functions of the RS-232 leads.

If documentation is not available, a device is available for monitoring the RS-232 leads. A *break-out box*, described in Appendix E, may be used to determine which leads are provided by a device. Connect the break-out box to the RS-232 port and make sure that the device is powered and the port in question is active or enabled. The lights on the break-out box should display which leads are being generated from the device. From this display a determination can generally be made as to whether the device is emulating DCE or DTE. For example, if either pin 20, data terminal ready, or pin 4, request to send, is on, the port is more than likely emulating data terminal equipment and is expecting to be connected to a modem or device emulating data communication equipment signals. On the other hand, if the display shows that signals such as clear to send, data set ready, or data carrier detect are present, the port is probably emulating data communication equipment and will allow a straight-through cable to be used when connecting a terminal configured as DTE, as if connecting to a modem.

If neither the documentation nor a break-out box is available, consult Appendix F of this text. The pin assignments with their corresponding directions are listed for a multitude of devices. From the direction of the pins, a determination can be

*Model 43 is a trademark of Teletype Corp.

†Apple II Plus is a trademark of Apple Computer.

‡Super Serial Card is a trademark of Apple Computer.

made as to how the device is configured. Should all these sources fail, consult the dealer or vendor who markets the product.

Another important aspect of RS-232 interfacing is whether the port is programmable or not. Programmability involves, among other things, the ability to change the directions of the leads. This may be optionable through software or may require some hardware jumpering on the I/O board that provides the port. This option may determine if a straight-through cable may be used by allowing the port to be configured to emulate either DTE or DCE. For example, when connecting a printer (DTE) to an optionable port, configure the port to emulate DCE, as this normally allows the use of a straight-through cable as opposed to a null-modem cable. If a modem is to be connected, configure the port as data terminal equipment to allow proper interaction of the signals. Once again, a straight-through cable may be used. If the port offers this flexibility, configure the port to best suit your environment.

Once the pin assignments and directions have been determined, consult Appendix G for a layout of the cables that may be built to interconnect two devices requiring cross connections. Many of the interconnections may be satisfied with a standard null-modem cable; other connections may require specialized cables. Many specialized cables are shown in Appendix G. It is important to note that not all the outlined pin connections in the appendix are required for the cables to work. They are merely provided for completeness. If your device is not listed in the appendix and you are attempting a connection, simply find a device in Appendix F that has the same pin configuration and use this device as a surrogate when referencing Appendix G.

Often, ports will provide signals generally used for testing purposes. These signals normally have a constant voltage on them, such as +12 volts or −12 volts. For example, some terminals have a positive voltage output on pin 9 of the interface. This lead may be very helpful in satisfying the requirements of the device to be attached.

Assume that a modem, to be connected to the terminal, requires pin 4 to be on before data may be transmitted. If the terminal doesn't provide pin 4 but does provide a positive voltage on pin 9, pin 9 may be crossed to pin 4, as depicted in Figure 8-5. This will maintain request to send (pin 4) and allow data transmission to occur. Modems may also provide signals like these and may be used to fulfill signal requirements in the same manner. The important factor is that all requirements of the ports, with regard to pins' being on or off, must be met.

The cable between the devices to be connected is important to successful implementation. However, after a cable has been built or supplied, a number of other

Terminal		Modem	
Function	Pin	Pin	Function
+12 volts	9 ——————▶ 4		Request to send

Figure 8-5

Item	Options
Speed	75 bps to 19,200 bps
Flow control	ETX/ACK, XON/XOFF, hardware
Parity	Odd, even, none
Character length	5,6,7,8
# of stop bits	1,1.5,2
Mode	Simplex, half/full duplex
Echoplex	Yes, no
Line feeds	0,1,2
Transmission mode	Async, sync, isochronous
Polarity	Positive, negative

Figure 8-6

items must be compared and set properly before the interfacing will be complete. Figure 8-6 provides a checklist for options generally found on computers and peripherals. Each element will be discussed as it relates to interfacing equipment.

Speed.   The port speed of both devices should be consistent to prevent data from being garbled. If the maximum rate of operation for a printer is 300 bits per second (bps), the device sending data to the printer must also be set at 300 bps. If both devices may transmit and receive at 4800 bps, set them both at 4800 bps. The speed of transmission through an RS-232 port becomes extremely important when a printer is involved, due to the aspects of buffering and flow control. Refer to the section on flow control for further explanation.

Flow Control.   Flow control, discussed in Chapter 6, involves the regulation of data transferred between two devices. Improper setting of this option could cause data to be lost, garbled, or not transmitted at all. Data flow must be regulated between devices such as a computer and a printer. Although both devices' transmission speeds are set the same, the speed of operation differs. The printer, because it is partially mechanical, may have a printing speed substantially less than the transmission speed, while the computer has the capability of transmitting at a much higher speed. Because of this, either the data must be buffered for delayed printing or flow control must occur to regulate when a printer is capable of receiving more data. For example, if the transmission speed is 4800 bps and each character has 10 bits, 480 characters per second (cps) are being transmitted by the computer (4800 divided by 10). However, the printer may be capable of printing only 100 cps. In these cases, flow control may be used to ensure that no loss of data occurs. Choices for flow control usually involve either XON/XOFF, ETX/ACK, or hardware via one of the RS-232 pins. As discussed in Chapter 6, XON/XOFF is a software flow control method in which characters are transmitted to indicate the status of the printer's condition. ETX/ACK, another software flow control scheme, is similar in concept to XON/XOFF. The connection of pins such as pins 11, 19, and 20 to a required input signal at the computer is termed *hardware flow control*. Flow control, used in conjunction with a buffer in the computer or printer, makes for a very efficient operation at maximum transmission speeds. With or without a buffer, flow control offers a means of overcoming the relatively slow operational speed of a printer. Other devices besides printers require flow control, but the concept is the same. The important aspect is that both ports are configured for the same flow-control method, software or hardware.

Parity.   Any of the parity types discussed in Chapter 2 are acceptable. Simply be consistent at both ends to prevent the garbling of data.

Character Length.   Another factor causing garbled data is the variation of character lengths. For example, there is a five-bit Baudot code and a seven-bit ASCII code. Regardless of the code, if parity is involved, determine if the character-length option includes the parity bit or not, and option accordingly at both ends. Be consistent.

Number of Stop Bits.   Ensure that the same stop bit length is selected at both ends. Check this option if garbled data appears sporadically. Chapter 2 describes the function of the stop bits. The selections are generally 1, 1.5, or 2. Choose the same number for both ends of the configuration.

Mode.   Generally, three modes of operation are available—simplex, half-duplex, and full-duplex. Selection should be consistent, as this option could determine which RS-232 signals are generated or monitored by a port. For example, if a printer is optioned for simplex mode (receive-only), pin 4 may not be generated. In a null-modem cable, this pin may be crossed to pin 8 at the computer end. If the computer requires pin 8 to be on before it will transmit, data transmission will never occur. Choose the mode that suits the environment, and option both ends accordingly.

Echoplex.   This option refers to the displaying of characters. Echoplex is closely related to the modes half- and full-duplex, and the terms are often used interchangeably by vendors to describe options. Some terminals have the option of either locally displaying characters as they are typed or leaving this up to the far end. The terminal may be optioned not to display the characters until they are ''echoed'' back from the far end, even though they are typed on the keyboard. If the far end is to echo the characters back to the originating device, this is termed *echoplexing*. By its very nature of operation, echoplexing implies that data will be both transmitted and received simultaneously (full-duplex). For example, if a CRT or terminal is connected to a computer that is optioned for echoplexing, a character typed at the keyboard is not displayed until the computer transmits it back. If you think of this in RS-232 terms, the characters that leave on pin 2, transmitted data, are not displayed until they are received on pin 3, received data. This may be used as a form of error detection. If the character displayed is not the same as the one typed, chances are that a parity error has occurred. The terminal operator can then backspace and retype the character.

The device that is to echo the characters should be optioned for echoplexing. As indicated, echoplexing is often confused with the duplexes. If a character is typed, such as *A,* and on the terminal appears *AA,* the far end is echoplexing while the terminal is optioned for local displaying of the characters as they are typed. Sometimes this is the half-duplex option. Half-duplex in this environment means that the terminal is locally generating the typed character. This, in conjunction with the far-end echoplexing, produces the double vision. Change the local terminal to full-duplex or the far end to no echoplexing to alleviate the problem. If, on the other hand, after an *A* is typed, nothing appears, the local device is probably optioned for full-duplex while the far end is not set up to echoplex. Change to half-duplex locally or to enable echoplexing at the far end to resolve the problem. Because they may not always be used interchangeably, the duplexes and echoplexing, as used in your devices, should be thoroughly understood for proper optioning.

Line Feeds.   This option generally offers three choices, 0, 1, or 2. Coordination between the two devices is in order to allow proper spacing on a terminal or printer. Generally, the devices may be optioned to perform a line feed upon the occurrence of a carriage return. If a computer transmits a carriage return to a terminal or printer only, the terminal will perform line feeds according to this option. An option of 0 in this circumstance will produce overwriting on the same line, as no vertical spacing takes place. If 1 is selected, single spacing will occur. Double spacing can be accomplished by selecting 2. Care should be taken in that the computer may already transmit a line feed along with a carriage return. In summary, if unwanted spacing occurs, this option should be checked.

Transmission Mode.   Three choices are generally available for this option: asynchronous, synchronous, or isochronous. Asynchronous implies that start and stop bits are required for timing purposes. In an asynchronous environment, be sure and check the number-of-stop-bits option. Synchronous transmission involves the use of clocks to transmit the data, as covered in Chapters 2 and 5. Option one of the devices in a synchronous environment to provide the timing and check that the proper leads are present in the cables. The third choice is *isochronous,* which is a combination of the other two. Data in an asynchronous format are transmitted synchronously. Ensure that both ends are optioned the same.

Polarity.   Polarity has to do with whether a signal is positive or negative. The importance of polarity is generally realized in the area of hardware flow control. For example, if pin 19 is used for the busy signal, an option may exist for the signal on pin 19 to be either positive or negative when the buffer of the device has room available for more data. A determination should be made for the transmitting device's requirements. If the transmitting device requires a positive voltage on the busy signal to enable transmission, option the printer (or receiving device) to generate a positive, or true, signal. Some devices require the reverse or a negative signal for this; however, a positive indication is generally used. Option accordingly.

As these explanations indicate, there are many considerations beyond RS-232 factors that are involved when interfacing serial devices. However, the cable connecting the RS-232 ports is a significant component of the configuration.

In summary, all items should be checked for proper optioning to permit a successful installation. Consult the various user's manuals to determine how to option for DTE or DCE emulation, speed, parity, flow control, character length, number of stop bits, transmission mode, and various other options. Use Appendixes F and G for aids in configuring the proper cable between devices.

For further technical information on the details of the RS-232 and other proposed and existing serial interfaces, such as RS-449, consult Appendixes A, B, and C. The electrical characteristics of the signals, as well as the maximum and minimum voltages allowed on the interfaces, can be found in the standards provided. Another source is John McNamara's *Technical Aspects of Data Communications*, listed in the bibliography.

We hope you enjoy interfacing with RS-232.

REVIEW QUESTIONS

1. Describe DTE emulation versus DCE emulation within an RS-232 port.
2. If data are being transmitted from a computer to a printer but are being garbled, what options should be checked?
3. If data are being lost or printed only sporadically, what options should be checked?
4. A VT-100 terminal operator types in an *M* and sees *MM* on the screen. Describe and solve the problem.
5. If an IBM PC is dumping data to a printer and the printer is double-spacing where it should only be single-spacing, explain the potential causes.

9

Answers
to Review
Questions

Chapter 2

1. asynchronous transmission
2. Simplex
3. nonsimultaneously, simultaneously
4. communications facilities *or* telephone lines
5. terminals, printers, computers
6. data terminal equipment
7. data communication equipment
8. RS-232
9. dial-up *or* switched
10. Private
11. Modem
12. modem
13. Signals
14. parity
15. start, stop

Chapter 3

1. 2, 3, received data
2. 22, ring indicator. No, it correlates to the ringing of the phone.
3. 20, data terminal ready
4. Data set ready will be high.
5. half-duplex (HDX)
6. 4, request to send; data carrier detect, clear to send
7. Request to send (pin 4)
8. Data terminal ready (pin 20)
9. 1
10. reference point, 7
11. Pin 2 is normally the lead used for characters output from the terminal to the modem, while the modem passes the characters it receives off the line to the terminal on pin 3, received data. When an intelligent modem is used, the pins serve the same function, as far as directions of data. What changes are the data. Between the modem and the terminal, the information necessary to dial and establish a connection is transferred. It is up to the modem to interpret the digits for dialing and supply the appropriate responses back to the terminal. A sample interaction on pins 2 and 3 might be as shown in Figure 9-1.

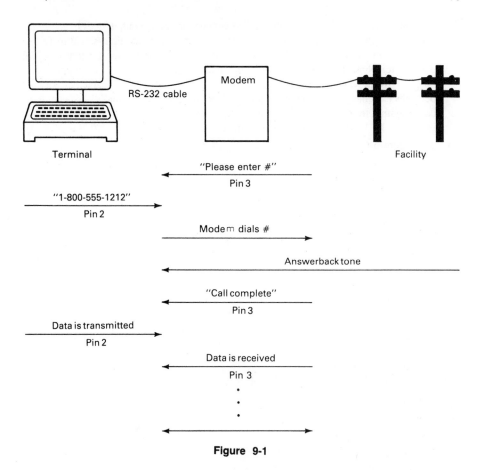

Figure 9-1

12. DTR, pin 20, is the RS-232 pin determining whether a call is maintained or not. When a terminal is in on-line mode, DTR is asserted. To disconnect, merely place the terminal off-line by either unplugging it, pressing a local mode button, or disabling the RS-232 port in some fashion. By placing the terminal in local mode, DTR is deasserted. The modem, upon detection of this, drops the call.

13. Autoanswer allows unattended operation at a computer or terminal site. Pin 20, DTR, allows the modem to answer the call if it is optioned for this feature. The way a modem knows that a call is arriving is by monitoring pin 22, ring indicator, which fluctuates with the ringing of the phone. Even if autoanswer is optioned in the modem and pin 22 indicates an incoming call, the modem will not answer the call unless pin 20 is on.

14. Reviewing the RS-232 signals, we find that upon entrance of data mode, either manually or automatically, the modem gives an output signal to the computer (DTE) indicating that a connection has been established. Once this occurs, the modem turns on pin 6, data set ready. The computer, upon detection of DSR high, knows it can transmit data across the dial-up connection and promptly prompts the promptee.

15. The golden rule when dealing with RS-232 connections is: An output goes to an input, and vice versa. For example, an output signal from DTE is an input signal to DCE. Transmitted data, output from DTE, are actually input to the modem for transmission over the telephone lines. At the far end, the modem receives the data and outputs them on pin 3 to the DTE. The DTE accepts them as input, or received data. Perspective becomes extremely important. Viewing pin 4, RTS, from the terminal's perspective, it carries output from the DTE. Viewing this same lead from the modem's angle, it carries input into DCE. Remember: Output to input, input to output.

16. See Figure 3-6.

Chapter 4

1. DSR (pin 6).
2. DSR is off.
3. False
4. False
5. True
6. See Figure 4-2.

Chapter 5

1. asynchronous transmission
2. synchronous transmission
3. buffering
4. timing
5. bits per second (bps)
6. 20,000
7. transmit, receive
8. 24; 15
9. 17
10. slave
11. The issue of internal versus external determines which leads will be used for the clock signal to drive the data. The complicating factor is whether the option of internal or external is being viewed from the perspective of the terminal or computer or the modem. This option is normally viewed from the modem's perspective.

    From the Modem's Perspective: With internal timing, the modem will provide to the DTE on pin 15 the rate at which data will be transmitted. With external timing, the modem will receive its transmit timing from the DTE on pin 24.

    From the Terminal's Perspective: With internal timing, the terminal will provide the clock rate to the DCE on pin 24. With external timing, the terminal will receive the transmitting rate from the DCE on pin 15.

12. Slave timing is a means of reducing the number of timing sources in a network. By deriving the transmit timing from a received signal, the number of clocks is limited,

which decreases the likelihood of errors that might normally occur with mismatched clocks. The transmit timing is said to be slaved off the receive timing.

13. Asynchronous transmission, also known as start/stop, is a scheme in which each character is individually timed, by the start and stop bits. Synchronous transmission is a scheme involving the buffering of data to be transmitted at a clock rate, determined by DTE or DCE, at a constant, predictable rate.

14. See Figure 5-6.

Chapter 6

1. primary
2. Secondary. XON/XOFF: An XOFF character is transmitted by the printer to indicate that it can't receive any more data. Once the printer problem condition clears, an XON character is transmitted. This is an indication to the computer that it can resume data transmission.
3. STD, SRD
4. SRTS, SCTS, SDCD/SRLSD
5. reverse channel
6. If the print speed is less than the transmission (port) speed and the buffer associated with the printer fills up, data could be lost unless a scheme is devised to tell the computer when to temporarily stop transmitting data. This can be accomplished by software or hardware. If both devices support software flow control, the XON/XOFF characters can be transmitted to start and stop data transmission. If XON/XOFF is not supported, reverse channel can be used as a hardware RS-232 flow-control mechanism.

Chapter 7

1. null-modem cable
2. Cross
3. synchronous modem eliminator
4. 50
5. ground, data, control, and timing
6. DTE
7. 1, 7
8. 3
9. CTS, 5, 8
10. 20, DSR
11. data set ready
12. 24
13. pins 24, 15, and 17
14. timing
15. Secondary request to send
16. The connections would be as shown in Figure 9-2. Don't connect pin 4 straight through at the printer end. Connect pin 19 from the printer to pin 4 at the modem. At the com-

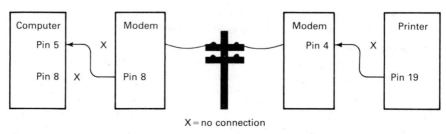

X = no connection

Figure 9.2

Figure 9-2

puter, don't connect pins 5 and 8 straight through. From the modem, connect pin 8 to pin 5 into the computer. As long as the printer at the far end has pin 19 on, indicating that it can receive data, this indication will be passed over to the computer via the RTS-DCD interaction. Because pin 8 is looped up to pin 5, this will give a clear-to-send indication back to the computer.

17. Output signal to input signal, input signal to output signal

Chapter 8

1. When a port is set up to emulate DTE, it is outputting the signals normally output by terminal equipment such as RTS, DTR, and SRTS. At the same time, it is expecting to receive the standard DCE input signals, such as CTS, DSR, and DCD, whereas a port set up as DCE is expecting to be attached to DTE. Signals like TD, RTS, and DTR are input signals, and RD, CTS, DSR, and DCD are output signals for the port.

2. speed, number of stop bits, parity, character length

3. XON/XOFF—either hardware or software, buffer size

4. Find out if the far-end computer is echoplexing. If so, set the VT-100 terminal option to full-duplex or whatever option eliminates the local echo. The local echo in conjunction with the echo causes the double image.

5. The computer board could be adding two line feeds (LF) to each carriage return (CR). Maybe the printer is adding the additional LF. If single spacing is desired, ensure that the computer or printer performs a line feed with each carriage return, but not both devices.

A

EIA

Standard

RS-232-C

This appendix contains extracts from the Electronic Industries Association RS-232-C Standard, which outlines the interface between data terminal equipment and data communication equipment employing serial binary data interchange. The standard, in its entirety, is available for order from the following address:

EIA Engineering Department
Standards Sales
2001 Eye Street, N.W.
Washington, D.C. 20006
(202) 457-4966

Notice

EIA engineering standards are designed to serve the public interest through eliminating misunderstandings between manufacturers and purchasers, facilitating interchangeability and improvement of products, and assisting the purchaser in selecting and obtaining with minimum delay the proper product for his particular need. Existence of such standards shall not in any respect preclude any member or nonmember of EIA from manufacturing or selling products not conforming to such standards, nor shall the existence of such standards preclude their voluntary use by those other than EIA members whether the standard is to be used either domestically or internationally.

Recommended standards are adopted by EIA without regard to whether or not their adoption may involve patents on articles, materials, or processes. By such action, EIA does not assume any liability to any patent owner, nor does it assume any obligation whatever to parties adopting recommended standards.

1.1   This standard is applicable to the interconnection of data terminal equipment (DTE) and data communication equipment (DCE) employing serial binary data interchange. It defines:

Section 2. Electrical Signal Characteristics
Electrical characteristics of the interchange signals and associated circuitry.

Section 3. Interface Mechanical Characteristics
Definition of the mechanical characteristics of the interface between the data terminal equipment and the data communication equipment.

Section 4. Functional Description of Interchange Circuits
Functional description of a set of data, timing, and control interchange circuits for use at a digital interface between data terminal equipment and data communication equipment.

Section 5. Standard Interfaces for Selected Communication System Configurations

Standard subsets of specific interchange circuits defined for a specific group of data communication system applications.

In addition, the standard includes:

Section 6. Recommendations and Explanatory Notes

Section 7. Glossary of New Terms

1.2   This standard includes thirteen specific interface configurations intended to meet the needs of fifteen defined system applications. These configurations are identified by type, using alphabetic characters A through M. In addition, type Z has been reserved for applications not covered by types A through M and where the configuration of interchange circuits is to be specified, in each case, by the supplier.

1.3   This standard is applicable for use at data signaling rates in the range from zero to a nominal upper limit of 20,000 bits per second.

1.4   This standard is applicable for the interchange of data, timing, and control signals when used in conjunction with electronic equipment, each of which has a single common return (signal ground), that can be interconnected at the interface point. It does not apply where electrical isolation between equipment on opposite sides of the interface point is required.

1.5   This standard applies to both synchronous and nonsynchronous serial binary data communication systems.

1.6   This standard applies to all classes of data communication service, including:

1.6.1   Dedicated leased or private-line service, either two-wire or four-wire. Consideration is given to both point-to-point and multipoint operation.

1.6.2   Switched-network service, either two-wire or four-wire. Consideration is given to automatic answering of calls; however, this standard does not include all of the interchange circuits required for automatically originating a connection. (See EIA Standard RS-366, "Interface Between Data Terminal Equipment and Automatic Calling Equipment for Data Communication.")

1.7   The data set may include transmitting and receiving signal converters as well as control functions. Other functions, such as pulse regeneration, error control, etc., may or may not be provided. Equipment to provide these additional functions may be included in the data terminal equipment or in the data communication equipment, or it may be implemented as a separate unit interposed between the two.

1.7.1   When such additional functions are provided within the data terminal equipment or the data communication equipment, this interface standard shall apply only to the interchange circuits between the two classes of equipment.

1.7.2   When additional functions are provided in a separate unit inserted between the data terminal equipment and the data communication equipment,
this standard shall apply to both sides (the interface with the data terminal
equipment and the interface with the data communication equipment. . .) of
such separate unit.

1.8   This standard applies to all of the modes of operation afforded under the
system configurations indicated in Section 5, Standard Interfaces for Selected Communication System Configurations.

Pin number	Circuit	Description
1	AA	Protective ground
2	BA	Transmitted data
3	BB	Received data
4	CA	Request to send
5	CB	Clear to send
6	CC	Data set ready
7	AB	Signal ground (common return)
8	CF	Received line signal detector
9	—	(Reserved for data set testing)
10	—	(Reserved for data set testing)
11		Unassigned
12	SCF	Secondary received line signal detector
13	SCB	Secondary clear to send
14	SBA	Secondary transmitted data
15	DB	Transmission signal element timing (DCE source)
16	SBB	Secondary received data
17	DD	Receiver signal element timing (DCE source)
18		Unassigned
19	SCA	Secondary request to send
20	CD	Data terminal ready
21	CG	Signal quality detector
22	CE	Ring indicator
23	CH/CI	Data signal rate selector (DTE/DCE source)
24	DA	Transmit signal element timing (DTE source)
25		Unassigned

Figure A–1   Interface Connector Pin Assignments

Interchange Circuits

Circuit AA: Protective Ground (CCITT 101)
Direction: Not applicable
This conductor shall be electrically bonded to the machine or equipment
frame. It may be further connected to external grounds as required by applicable
regulations.

Circuit AB: Signal Ground or Common Return (CCITT 102)
Direction: Not applicable

This conductor establishes the common ground reference potential for all interchange circuits except Circuit AA (Protective Ground). Within the data communication equipment, this circuit shall be brought to one point, and it shall be possible to connect this point to Circuit AA by means of a wire strap inside the equipment. This wire strap can be connected or removed at installation, as may be required to meet applicable regulations or to minimize the introduction of noise into electronic circuitry.

Circuit BA: Transmitted Data (CCITT 103)
Direction: TO data communication equipment
Signals on this circuit are generated by the data terminal equipment and are transferred to the local transmitting signal converter for transmission of data to remote data terminal equipment.

The data terminal equipment shall hold Circuit BA (Transmitted Data) in marking condition during intervals between characters or words, and at all times when no data are being transmitted.

In all systems, the data terminal equipment shall not transmit data unless an ON condition is present on all of the following four circuits, where implemented.

1. Circuit CA (Request to Send)
2. Circuit CB (Clear to Send)
3. Circuit CC (Data Set Ready)
4. Circuit CD (Data Terminal Ready)

All data signals that are transmitted across the interface on interchange circuit BA (Transmitted Data) during the time an ON condition is maintained on all of the above four circuits, where implemented, shall be transmitted to the communication channel. . . .

Circuit BB: Received Data (CCITT 104)
Direction: FROM data communication equipment
Signals on this circuit are generated by the receiving signal converter in response to data signals received from remote data terminal equipment via the remote transmitting signal converter. Circuit BB (Received Data) shall be held in the Binary One (Marking) condition at all times when Circuit CF (Received Line Signal Detector) is in the OFF condition.

On a half-duplex channel, Circuit BB shall be held in the Binary One (Marking) condition when Circuit CA (Request to Send) is in the ON condition and for a brief interval following the ON to OFF transition of Circuit CA to allow for the completion of transmission (see Circuit BA, Transmitted Data) and the decay of line reflections. . . .

Circuit CA: Request to Send (CCITT 105)
Direction: TO data communication equipment
This circuit is used to condition the local data communication equipment for

data transmission and, on a half-duplex channel, to control the direction of data transmission of the local data communication equipment.

On one-way-only channels or duplex channels, the ON condition maintains the data communication equipment in the transmit mode. The OFF condition maintains the data communication equipment in a nontransmit mode.

On a half-duplex channel, the ON condition maintains the data communication equipment in the transmit mode and inhibits the receive mode. The OFF condition maintains the data communication equipment in the receive mode.

A transition from OFF to ON instructs the data communication equipment to enter the transmit code. . . . The data communication equipment responds by taking such action as may be necessary and indicates completion of such actions by turning ON Circuit CB (Clear to Send), thereby indicating to the data terminal equipment that data may be transferred across the interface point on interchange Circuit BA (Transmitted Data).

A transition from ON to OFF instructs the data communication equipment to complete the transmission of all data which was previously transferred across the interface point on interchange Circuit BA and then assume a nontransmit mode or a receive mode, as appropriate. The data communication equipment responds to this instruction by turning OFF Circuit CB (Clear to Send) when it is prepared to respond again to a subsequent ON condition of Circuit CA.

Note: A nontransmit mode does not imply that all line signals have been removed from the communication channel. . . .

When Circuit CA is turned OFF, it shall not be turned ON again until Circuit CB has been turned OFF by the data communication equipment.

An ON condition is required on Circuit CA as well as on Circuit CB, Circuit CC (Data Set Ready), and, where implemented, Circuit CD (Data Terminal Ready) whenever the data terminal equipment transfers data across the interface on interchange Circuit BA.

It is permissible to turn Circuit CA ON at any time when Circuit CB is OFF regardless of the condition of any other interchange circuit.

Circuit CB: Clear to Send (CCITT 106)
Direction: FROM data communication equipment
Signals on this circuit are generated by the data communication equipment to indicate whether or not the data set is ready to transmit data.

The ON condition, together with the ON condition on interchange circuits CA, CC, and, where implemented, CD, is an indication to the data terminal equipment that signals presented on Circuit BA (Transmitted Data) will be transmitted to the communication channel.

The OFF condition is an indication to the data terminal equipment that it should not transfer data across the interface on interchange Circuit BA.

The ON condition of Circuit CB is a response to the occurrence of a simultaneous ON condition on Circuit CC (Data Set Ready) and Circuit CA (Request to Send), delayed as may be appropriate to the data communication equipment for es-

tablishing a data communication channel (including the removal
clamp from the Received Data interchange circuit of the remote da.
data terminal equipment.

Where Circuit CA (Request to Send) is not implemented in the dau.
cation equipment with transmitting capability, Circuit CA shall be assume
the ON condition at all times, and Circuit CB shall respond accordingly.

Circuit CC: Data Set Ready (CCITT 107)
Direction: FROM data communication equipment
Signals on this circuit are used to indicate the status of the local data set.
The ON condition on this circuit is presented to indicate [all of the following]:

1. The local data communication equipment is connected to a communication
   channel (''Off Hook'' in switched service).
2. The local data communication equipment is not in test (local or remote), talk
   (alternate voice), or dial* mode. . . .
3. The local data communication equipment has completed, where applicable:
   a. any timing functions required by the switching system to complete call establishment, and;
   b. the transmission of any discreet answer tone, the duration of which is
   controlled solely by the local data set.

Where the local data communication equipment does not transmit an answer
tone, or where the duration of the answer tone is controlled by some action of the
remote data set, the ON condition is presented as soon as all the other listed conditions (1, 2, and 3a) are satisfied.

This circuit shall be used only to indicate the status of the local data set. The
ON condition shall not be interpreted as either an indication that a communication
channel has been established to a remote data station or the status of any remote
station equipment.

The OFF condition shall appear at all other times and shall be an indication
that the data terminal equipment is to disregard signals appearing on any other interchange circuit with the exception of Circuit CE (Ring Indicator). The OFF condition
shall not impair the operation of Circuit CE or Circuit CD (Data Terminal Ready).

When the OFF condition occurs during the progress of a call before Circuit
CD is turned OFF, the data terminal equipment shall interpret this as a lost or
aborted connection and take action to terminate the call. Any subsequent ON condition on Circuit CC is to be considered a new call.

When the data set is used in conjunction with automatic calling equipment
(ACE), the OFF to ON transition of Circuit CC shall not be interpreted as an indica-

---

*The data communication equipment is considered to be in the dial mode when circuitry directly
associated with the call-origination function is connected to the communication channel. These functions
include signaling to the central office (dialing) and monitoring the communication channel for call progress or answer-back signals.

tion that the ACE has relinquished control of the communication channel to the data set. Indication of this is given on the appropriate lead in the ACE interface (see EIA Standard RS-366).

> *Note:* Attention is called to the fact that if a data call is interrupted by alternate voice communication, Circuit CC will be in the OFF condition during the time that voice communication is in progress. The transmission or reception of the signals required to condition the communication channel or data communication equipment in response to the ON condition of interchange Circuit CA (Request to Send) of the transmitting data terminal equipment will take place after Circuit CC comes ON, but prior to the ON condition on Circuit CB (Clear to Send) or Circuit CF (Received Line Signal Detector).

Circuit CD: Data Terminal Ready (CCITT 108.2)
Direction: TO data communication equipment

Signals on this circuit are used to control switching of the data communication equipment to the communication channel. The ON condition prepares the data communication equipment to be connected to the communication channel and maintains the connection established by external means (e.g., manual call origination, manual answering, or automatic call origination).

When the station is equipped for automatic answering of received calls and is in the automatic answering mode, connection to the line occurs only in response to a combination of a ringing signal and the ON condition of circuit CD (Data Terminal Ready); however, the data terminal equipment is normally permitted to present the ON condition on Circuit CD whenever it is ready to transmit or receive data, except as indicated below.

The OFF condition causes the data communication equipment to be removed from the communication channel following the completion of any "in process" transmission. See Circuit BA (Transmitted Data). The OFF condition shall not disable the operation of Circuit CE (Ring Indicator).

In switched-network applications, when Circuit CD is turned OFF, it shall not be turned ON again until Circuit CC (Data Set Ready) is turned OFF by the data communication equipment.

Circuit CE: Ring Indicator (CCITT 125)
Direction: FROM data communication equipment

The ON condition of this circuit indicates that a ringing signal is being received on the communication channel.

The ON condition shall appear approximately coincident with the ON segment of the ringing cycle (during rings) on the communication channel.

The OFF condition shall be maintained during the OFF segment of the ringing cycle (between "rings") and at all other times when ringing is not being received. The operation of this circuit shall not be disabled by the OFF condition on Circuit CD (Data Terminal Ready).

Circuit CF: Received Line Signal Detector (CCITT 109)
Direction: FROM data communication equipment

The ON condition on this circuit is presented when the data communication equipment is receiving a signal which meets its suitability criteria. These criteria are established by the data communication equipment manufacturer.

The OFF condition indicates that no signal is being received or that the received signal is unsuitable for demodulation.

The OFF condition of Circuit CF (Received Line Signal Detector) shall cause Circuit BB (Received Data) to be clamped to the Binary One (Marking) condition.

The indications on this circuit shall follow the actual onset or loss of signal by appropriate guard delays.

On half-duplex channels, Circuit CF is held in the OFF condition whenever Circuit CA (Request to Send) is in the ON condition and for a brief interval of time following the ON to OFF transition of Circuit CA. (See Circuit BB.)

Circuit CG: Signal Quality Detector (CCITT 110)
Direction: FROM data communication equipment

Signals on this circuit are used to indicate whether or not there is a high probability of an error in the received data.

An ON condition is maintained whenever there is no reason to believe that an error has occurred.

An OFF condition indicates that there is a high probability of an error. It may, in some instances, be used to call automatically for the retransmission of the previously transmitted data signal. Preferably the response of this circuit shall be such as to permit identification of individual questionable signal elements on Circuit BB (Received Data).

Circuit CH: Data Signal Rate Selector (DTE Source) (CCITT 111)
Direction: TO data communication equipment

Signals on this circuit are used to select between the two data signaling rates in the case of dual rate synchronous data sets or the two ranges of data signaling rates in the case of dual range nonsynchronous data sets.

An ON condition shall select the higher data signaling rate or range of rates.

The rate of timing signals, if included in the interface, shall be controlled by this circuit as may be appropriate.

Circuit CI: Data Signal Rate Selector (DCE Source) (CCITT 112)
Direction: FROM data communication equipment

Signals on this circuit are used to select between the two data signaling rates in the case of dual rate synchronous data sets or the two ranges of data signaling rates in the case of dual range nonsynchronous data sets.

An ON condition shall select the higher data signaling rate or range of rates.

The rate of timing signals, if included in the interface, shall be controlled by this circuit as may be appropriate.

Circuit DA: Transmitter Signal Element Timing (DTE Source) (CCITT 113)
Direction: TO data communication equipment

Signals on this circuit are used to provide the transmitting signal converter with signal element timing information.

The ON to OFF transition shall nominally indicate the center of each signal element on Circuit BA (Transmitted Data). When Circuit DA is implemented in the DTE, the DTE shall normally provide timing information on this circuit whenever the DTE is in a power ON condition. It is permissible for the DTE to withhold timing information on this circuit for short periods provided Circuit CA (Request to Send) is in the OFF condition. (For example, the temporary withholding of timing information may be necessary in performing maintenance tests within the DTE.)

Circuit DB: Transmitter Signal Element Timing (DCE Source) (CCITT 114)
Direction: FROM data communication equipment

Signals on this circuit are used to provide the data terminal equipment with signal element timing information. The data terminal equipment shall provide a data signal on Circuit BA (Transmitted Data) in which the transitions between signal elements nominally occur at the time of the transitions from OFF to ON condition of the signal on Circuit DB. When Circuit DB is implemented in the DCE, the DCE shall normally provide timing information on this circuit whenever the DCE is in a power ON condition. It is permissible for the DCE to withhold timing information on this circuit for short periods provided Circuit CC (Data Set Ready) is in the OFF condition. (For example, the withholding of timing information may be necessary in performing maintenance tests within the DCE.)

Circuit DD: Receiver Signal Element Timing (DCE Source) (CCITT 115)
Direction: FROM data communication equipment

Signals on this circuit are used to provide the data terminal equipment with received signal element timing information. The transition from ON to OFF condition shall nominally indicate the center of each signal element on Circuit BB (Received Data). Timing information on Circuit DD shall be provided at all times when Circuit CF (Received Line Signal Detector) is in the ON condition. It may, but need not, be present following the ON to OFF transition of Circuit CF...

Circuit SBA: Secondary Transmitted Data (CCITT 118)
Direction: TO data communication equipment

This circuit is equivalent to Circuit BA (Transmitted Data) except that it is used to transmit data via the secondary channel.

Signals on this circuit are generated by the data terminal equipment and are connected to the local secondary channel transmitting signal converter for transmission of data to remote data terminal equipment.

The data terminal equipment shall hold Circuit SBA (Secondary Transmitted Data) in marking condition during intervals between characters or words and at all times when no data are being transmitted.

In all systems, the data terminal equipment shall not transmit data on the secondary channel unless an ON condition is present on all of the following four circuits, where implemented:

1. Circuit SCA (Secondary Request to Send)
2. Circuit SCB (Secondary Clear To Send)
3. Circuit CC (Data Set Ready)
4. Circuit CD (Data Terminal Ready)

All data signals that are transmitted across the interface on interchange Circuit SBA during the time when the above conditions are satisfied shall be transmitted to the communication channel...

When the secondary channel is usable only for circuit assurance or to interrupt the flow of data in the primary channel (less than 10 baud capability), Circuit SBA (Secondary Transmitted Data) is normally not provided, and the channel carrier is turned ON or OFF by means of Circuit SCA (Secondary Request to Send). Carrier OFF is interpreted as an interrupt condition.

Circuit SBB: Secondary Received Data (CCITT 119)
Direction: FROM data communication equipment
This circuit is equivalent to Circuit BB (Received Data) except that it is used to receive data on the secondary channel.

When the secondary channel is usable only for circuit assurance or to interrupt the flow of data in the primary channel, Circuit SBB is normally not provided. See interchange Circuit SCF (Secondary Received Line Signal Detector).

Circuit SCA: Secondary Request to Send (CCITT 120)
Direction: TO data communication equipment
This circuit is equivalent to Circuit CA (Request to Send) except that it requests the establishment of the secondary channel instead of requesting the establishment of the primary data channel.

Where the secondary channel is used as a backward channel, the ON condition of Circuit CA (Request to Send) shall disable Circuit SCA and it shall not be possible to condition the secondary channel transmitting signal converter to transmit during any time interval when the primary channel transmitting signal converter is so conditioned. Where system considerations dictate that one or the other of the two channels be in transmit mode at all times but never both simultaneously, this can be accomplished by permanently applying an ON condition to Circuit SCA (Secondary Request to Send) and controlling both the primary and secondary channels, in complementary fashion, by means of Circuit CA (Request to Send). Alternatively, in this case, Circuit SCB need not be implemented in the interface.

When the secondary channel is usable only for circuit assurance or to interrupt the flow of data in the primary data channel, Circuit SCA shall serve to turn ON the secondary channel unmodulated carrier. The OFF condition of Circuit SCA shall turn OFF the secondary channel carrier and thereby signal an interrupt condition at the remote end of the communication channel.

Circuit SCB: Secondary Clear to Send (CCITT 121)

Direction: FROM data communication equipment

This circuit is equivalent to Circuit CB (Clear to Send) except that it indicates the availability of the secondary channel instead of indicating the availability of the primary channel. This circuit is not provided where the secondary channel is usable only as a circuit assurance or an interrupt channel.

Circuit SCF: Secondary Received Line Signal Detector (CCITT 122)

Direction: FROM data communication equipment

This circuit is equivalent to Circuit CF (Received Line Signal Detector) except that it indicates the proper reception of the secondary channel line signal instead of indicating the proper reception of a primary channel received-line signal.

Where the secondary channel is usable only as a circuit assurance or an interrupt channel (see Circuit SCA, Secondary Request to Send), Circuit SCF shall be used to indicate the circuit assurance status or to signal the interrupt. The ON condition shall indicate circuit assurance or a noninterrupt condition. The OFF condition shall indicate circuit failure (no assurance) or the interrupt condition.

APPENDIX

B

EIA
Standard
RS-449

This appendix contains parts of the Electronic Industries Association RS-449 Standard, which outlines the general-purpose 37-position and 9-position interface for equipment employing serial binary data interchange. The actual standard may be ordered from:

EIA Engineering Department
Standards Sales
2001 Eye Street, N.W.
Washington, D.C. 20006
(202) 457-4966

Notice

EIA engineering standards are designed to serve the public interest through eliminating misunderstandings between manufacturers and purchasers, facilitating interchangeability and improvement of products, and assisting the purchaser in selecting and obtaining with minimum delay the proper product for his particular need. Existence of such standards shall not in any respect preclude any member or nonmember of EIA from manufacturing or selling products not conforming to such standards, nor shall the existence of such standards preclude their voluntary use by those other than EIA members whether the standard is to be used either domestically or internationally.

Recommended standards are adopted by EIA without regard to whether or not their adoption may involve patents on articles, materials, or processes. By such action, EIA does not assume any liability to any patent owner, nor does it assume any obligation whatever to parties adopting recommended standards.

EIA Standard RS-449 was developed in close coordination and cooperation with the international standards activities of the CCITT (International Telegraph and Telephone Consultative Committee) and ISO (International Organization for Standardization) and is compatible with CCITT Recommendation V.24, "List of Definitions for Interchange Circuits Between Data Terminal Equipment and Data Circuit–Terminating Equipment," and Recommendation V.54, "Loop Test Devices for Modems," as well as with ISO Draft Proposal DP-4902, "37-Pin and 9-Pin DTE/DCE Interface Connectors and Pin Assignments."

General-Purpose, 37-Position and 9-Position Interface for Data Terminal Equipment and Data Circuit–Terminating Equipment Employing Serial Binary Data Interchange

Foreword (This Foreword provides additional information and does not form an integral part of the EIA Standard specifying the General-Purpose 37-Position and 9-Position Interface for Data Terminal Equipment and Data Circuit-Terminating Equipment Employing Serial Binary Data Interchange.)

This Standard, together with EIA Standards RS-422 and RS-423, is intended to gradually replace EIA Standard RS-232-C as the specification for the interface between data terminal equipment (DTE) and data circuit-terminating equipment (DCE) employing serial binary data interchange. With a few additional provisions for interoperability, equipment conforming to this standard can interoperate with equipment designed to RS-232-C. This standard is intended primarily for data applications using analog telecommunications networks.

EIA Standard RS-232-C is in need of replacement in order to specify new electrical characteristics and to define several new interchange circuits. New electrical characteristics are needed to accommodate advances in integrated circuit design, to reduce crosstalk between interchange circuits, to permit greater distances between equipments, and to permit higher data signaling rates. With the expected increase in use of standard electrical interface characteristics between many different kinds of equipment, it is now appropriate to publish the electrical interface characteristics in separate standards. Two electrical interface standards have been published for voltage digital interface circuits:

EIA Standard RS-422 "Electrical Characteristics of Balanced-Voltage Digital Interface Circuits"

EIA Standard RS-423, "Electrical Characteristics of Unbalanced-Voltage Digital Interface Circuits"

With the adoption of EIA Standards RS-422 and RS-423, it became necessary to create a new standard which specifies the remaining characteristics (i.e., the functional and mechanical characteristics) of the interface between data terminal equipment and data circuit–terminating equipment. That is the purpose of this standard.

The basic interchange circuit functional definitions of EIA Standard RS-232-C have been retained in this standard. However, there are a number of significant differences:

1. Application of this standard has been expanded to include signaling rates up to 2,000,000 bits per second.

2. Ten circuit functions have been defined in this standard which were not part of RS-232-C. These include three circuits for control and status of testing functions in the DCE (Circuit LL, Local Loopback; Circuit RL, Remote Loopback; and Circuit TM, Test Mode), two circuits for control and status of the transfer of the DCE to a standby channel (Circuit SS, Select Standby, and Circuit SB, Standby Indicator), a circuit to provide an out-of-service function under control of the DTE (Circuit IS, Terminal In Service), a circuit to provide a new signal function (Circuit NS, New Signal), and a circuit for DCE frequency selection (Circuit SF, Select Frequency). In addition, two circuits have been defined to provide a common reference for each direction of transmission across the interface (Circuit SC, Send Common, and Circuit RC, Receive Common).

3. Three interchange circuits defined in RS-232-C have not been included in this standard. Protective ground (RS-232-C Circuit AA) is not included as part of the interface to permit bonding of equipment frames, when necessary, to be done in a manner which is in compliance with national and local electrical codes. However, a contact on the interface connector is assigned to facilitate the use of shielded interconnecting cable. The two circuits reserved for data set testing (RS-232-C contacts 9 and 10) have not been included in order to minimize the size of the interface connector.

4. Some changes have been made to the circuit function definitions. For example, operation of the Data Set Ready circuit has been changed and a new name, Data Mode, has been established due to the inclusion of a separate interchange circuit (Test Mode) to indicate a DCE test condition.

5. A new set of standard interfaces for selected communication system configurations has been established. In order to achieve a greater degree of standardization, the option in RS-232-C which permitted the omission of the Request to Send interchange circuit for certain transmit only or duplex primary channel applications has been eliminated.

6. A new set of circuit names and mnemonics has been established. To avoid confusion with RS-232-C, all mnemonics in this standard are different from those used in RS-232-C. The new mnemonics were chosen to be easily related to circuit functions and circuit names.

7. A different interface connector size and interface connector latching arrangement have been specified. A larger-size connector (37-position) is specified to accommodate the additional interface leads required for the ten newly defined circuit functions and to accommodate balanced operation for ten interchange circuits. In addition, a separate 9-position connector is specified to accommodate the secondary channel interchange circuits. The 37-position and 9-position connectors are from the same connector family as the 25-position connector in general use by equipment conforming to EIA Standard RS-232-C. A connector latching block is specified to permit latching and unlatching of the connectors without the use of a tool. This latching block will

also permit the use of screws to fasten together the connectors. The different connectors will also serve as an indication that certain precautions with regard to interface voltage levels, signal risetimes, fail-safe circuitry, grounding, etc., must be taken into account before equipment conforming to RS-232-C can be connected to equipment conforming to the new electrical characteristic standards. The connector contact assignments have been chosen to facilitate connection of equipment conforming to this standard to equipment conforming to RS-232-C.

Close attention was given during the development of RS-449 and RS-423 to facilitate an orderly transition from the existing RS-232-C equipment to the next generation without forcing obsolescence or costly retrofits. It will therefore be pos-

Circuit mnemonic	Circuit name	Circuit direction	Circuit type	
SG	Signal ground	—	Common	
SC	Send common	To DCE		
RC	Receive common	From DCE		
IS	Terminal in service	To DCE	Control	
IC	Incoming call	From DCE		
TR	Terminal ready	To DCE		
DM	Data mode	From DCE		
SD	Send data	To DCE	Data	Primary channel
RD	Receive data	From DCE		
TT	Terminal timing	To DCE	Timing	
ST	Send timing	From DCE		
RT	Receive timing	From DCE		
RS	Request to send	To DCE	Control	
CS	Clear to send	From DCE		
RR	Receiver ready	From DCE		
SQ	Signal quality	From DCE		
NS	New signal	To DCE		
SF	Select frequency	To DCE		
SR	Signaling rate selector	To DCE		
SI	Signaling rate indicator	From DCE		
SSD	Secondary send data	To DCE	Data	Secondary channel
SRD	Secondary receive data	From DCE		
SRS	Secondary request to send	To DCE	Control	
SCS	Secondary clear to send	From DCE		
SRR	Secondary receiver ready	From DCE		
LL	Local loopback	To DCE	Control	
RL	Remote loopback	To DCE		
TM	Test mode	From DCE		
SS	Select standby	To DCE	Control	
SB	Standby indicator	From DCE		

Figure B–1   Interchange Circuits

sible to connect new equipment designed to RS-449 on one side of an interface to equipment designed to RS-232-C on the other side of the interface. Such interconnections can be accomplished with a few additional provisions associated only with the new RS-449 equipment. These provisions are discussed in an EIA Industrial Electronics Bulletin (IE Bulletin No. 12), "Application Notes on Interconnection Between Interface Circuits Using RS-449 and RS-232-C."

This standard is designed to be compatible with the specifications of the International Telegraph and Telephone Consultative Committee (CCITT) and the International Organization for Standardization (ISO). However, it should be noted that this standard contains a few specifications which are subjects of further study in CCITT and ISO. These are:

1. Use of interchange circuits Terminal In Service and New Signal.
2. Status of interchange circuits during an equalizer retraining period.

The USA is actively participating in CCITT and ISO to gain international agreement on these items.

Work is presently underway, in cooperation with CCITT and ISO, to expand the Remote Loopback test function to include testing on multipoint networks. This augmentation will not affect the point-to-point testing capability specified in this document. Work is also underway to augment this standard to cover direct DTE-to-DTE applications. This augmentation will not affect, in any way, the DTE-to-DCE operation specified in this document. In addition, work will proceed in cooperation with CCITT toward the development of a more efficient all-balanced interface which minimizes the number of interchange circuits. It is expected that RS-449 will provide the basis for this new work.

APPENDIX

C

Industrial Electronics Bulletin No. 12

This appendix contains extracts from the application notes on interconnection between interface circuits using RS-449 and RS-232-C. It may be ordered from:

EIA Engineering Department
Standards Sales
2001 Eye Street, N.W.
Washington, D.C. 20006
(202) 457-4966

Introduction

The new series of digital interface standards, RS-449, RS-422, and RS-423, have been developed to meet the advancing state of the art and greatly enhance the operation between DTEs and DCEs for data communication applications. Since RS-232-C has been the pervasive digital interface standard for a number of years, close attention was given during the development of RS-449, RS-422, and RS-423 to the selection of parameter values that would facilitate an orderly transition from the existing RS-232-C equipment to the next generation without forcing obsolescence or costly retrofits. It will, therefore, be possible to connect new equipment designed to RS-449 on one side of an interface to equipment designed to RS-232-C on the other side of the interface. Such interconnection can be accomplished with a few additional provisions associated only with the new RS-449 equipment, and the performance will be that normally experienced between RS-232-C DTEs and DCEs.

This Industrial Electronics Bulletin provides application notes as guidance for implementing the necessary provisions that will allow continued use of existing RS-232-C equipment by facilitating a graceful transition to the new equipment using RS-449. [See Figure C-1].

RS-449		RS-232-C	
		AA	Protective ground
SG	Signal ground	AB	Signal ground
SC	Send common		
RC	Receive common		
IS	Terminal in service		
IC	Incoming call	CE	Ring indicator
TR*	Terminal ready	CD	Data terminal ready
DM*	Data mode	CC	Data set ready
SD*	Send data	BA	Transmitted data
RD*	Receive data	BB	Received data
TT*	Terminal timing	DA	Transmitter signal element timing (DTE source)
ST*	Send timing	DB	Transmitter signal element timing (DCE source)
RT*	Receive timing	DD	Receiver signal element timing
RS*	Request to send	CA	Request to send
CS*	Clear to send	CB	Clear to send
RR*	Receiver ready	CF	Received line signal detector
SQ	Signal quality	CG	Signal quality detector
NS	New signal		
SF	Select frequency		
SR	Signaling rate selector	CH	Data signal rate selector (DTE source)
SI	Signaling rate indicator	CI	Data signal rate selector (DCE source)
SSD	Secondary send data	SBA	Secondary transmitted data
SRD	Secondary receive data	SBB	Secondary received data
SRS	Secondary request to send	SCA	Secondary request to send
SCS	Secondary clear to send	SCB	Secondary clear to send
SRR	Secondary receiver ready	SCF	Secondary received line signal detector
LL	Local loopback		
RL	Remote loopback		
TM	Test mode		
			Pins 9 & 10 test function
SS	Select standby		
SB	Standby indicator		

*Category I circuits

Figure C–1 Equivalency Table

D

RS-232

Circuit Summary

with CCITT

Equivalents

Pin	Interchange Circuit	CCITT Equivalent	Description	Gnd	Data From DCE	Data To DCE	Control From DCE	Control To DCE	Timing From DCE	Timing To DCE
1	AA	101	Protective ground	X						
7	AB	102	Signal ground/common return	X						
2	BA	103	Transmitted data			X				
3	BB	104	Received data		X					
4	CA	105	Request to send					X		
5	CB	106	Clear to send				X			
6	CC	107	Data set ready				X			
20	CD	108.2	Data terminal ready					X		
22	CE	125	Ring indicator				X			
8	CF	109	Received line signal detector				X			
21	CG	110	Signal quality detector				X			
23	CH	111	Data signal rate selector (DTE)					X		
23	CI	112	Data signal rate selector (DCE)				X			
24	DA	113	Transmitter signal element timing (DTE)							X
15	DB	114	Transmitter signal element timing (DCE)						X	
17	DD	115	Receiver signal element timing (DCE)						X	
14	SBA	118	Secondary transmitted data			X				
16	SBB	119	Secondary received data		X					
19	SCA	120	Secondary request to send					X		
13	SCB	121	Secondary clear to send				X			
12	SCF	122	Secondary received line signal detector				X			

Figure D–1 RS-232 Circuit Summary With CCITT Equivalents

APPENDIX

E

Tools
of the Trade

The RS-232 serial interface leads and their functions should now be very familiar to you. The ground, data, control, and timing leads all relate in a logical fashion, as described in the text. But often the description simply is not enough. Is there any way actually to view this logical interaction of the leads? How can a user or service technician monitor the status of a given lead? This appendix explains the different tools available for use on the RS-232-C interface. These tools are available from a multitude of vendors and are offered in many different forms. Consult the ads in various periodicals for actual costs and availability of these devices and cables.

Break-Out Box

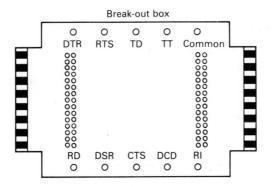

Figure E-1

Description and functions:

- RS-232 connector(s), both male and female
- LEDs for various RS-232 leads (DSR, DTR, TD, etc.)
- Jumper position for cross connections
- Possibly battery powered
- Allows monitoring of various RS-232 leads to detect whether they are high/low or on/off.
- By connecting this device to an RS-232 interface, one can determine if the port is wired for DCE or DTE emulation.
- Allows for opening of individual pin circuits
- Typical price is $125.

RS-232 Male/Female Adapter

Description and functions:

- Allows connection of mismatched RS-232-C connectors
- Changes male connector to female connector, or vice versa
- Typical price is $50.

RS-232 ABC/EIA Switch

Description and functions:

- Box with multiple RS-232 ports
- Usually no power is required.
- Allows interconnection of more than two serial devices
- Switch(es) for changing configuration without changing cables
- Can reduce the number of ports or devices required (e.g., two printers can share the same computer by the mere flip of a switch; also, two computers can share the one modem or printer with the same ease)
- Typical price is $100.

RS-232 Pin Inserter and Extractor

Description and functions:

- Allows easy insertion and extraction of crimped pins in a connector
- Typical price is $3.

RS-232 Synchronous Modem Eliminator

Description and functions:

- Box with two RS-232 connectors
- Usually AC-powered
- Replaces synchronous modems between two devices
- Provides clock for timing
- Provides null-modem cable function
- Typical price is $300.

RS-232 Cable Tester

Description and functions:

- Provides testing of RS-232 cables
- Indicates whether pins are wired straight through or possibly crossed over, as in a null-modem cable
- Typical price is $450.

RS-232 Buffer

Description and functions:

- Provides buffering or spooling of data (Buffers data being output to a slow-speed printer to free up a computer. The printer can then print at its own speed. This utilizes the computer resource better by allowing other functions to occur simultaneously with the printing operation.)
- Price varies from $150 to $1000, depending on the amount of buffer storage provided.

RS-232 Serial-to-Parallel Adapter

Description and functions:

- Box with serial and parallel cables attached
- Buffered for greater flexibility
- Allows parallel device—for example, a printer—to be connected to an RS-232 serial interface
- Typical price is $125.

RS-232/RS-449 Adapter

Description and functions:

- Converts pins from the RS-232 standard to the new RS-449 standard interface
- Allows devices with RS-232 interfaces to be connected to RS-449 ports
- Typical price is $50.

Although there are many more devices available to supplement the support of equipment incorporating an RS-232 interface, these should give you an idea of the array of "tools of the trade" that are available when working with the serial interfaces.

F

RS-232
Pin Assignments
for Computers
and Peripherals

Included in this appendix are computers, printers, and terminals (CRTs). Charts displaying RS-232-C pin assignments, along with their functions and directions, are available for the ports offered on the various devices. In addition, pertinent facts relating to items such as flow control are included. These items are extremely important when connecting combinations of computers, modems, and peripherals.

From these listings, a determination can be made for the construction of an RS-232 cable for connecting equipment. Once the devices have been selected, note the corresponding pin configuration. Use this pin configuration in conjunction with Appendix G to build the appropriate cable.

Every attempt was made to include as many different devices and accurate pin configurations as possible. However, should a device not be included, merely match its RS-232 configuration with one that is listed. Note the corresponding pin configuration and use this for a reference in Appendix G.

Company: Addmaster Corp.
Product: 170/180 Printers
Port: RS232   Pin Configuration: P02

Pin	Function	Direction
1	Chassis ground	N/A*
3	Received data	To printer
4	Request to send	From printer
5	Clear to send	To printer
7	Signal ground	N/A

Company: Adds, Inc.
Product: Multivision Computer
Port: Console   Pin Configuration: C02

Pin	Function	Direction
1	Ground	N/A
2	EIA in	To Multivision
3	EIA out	From Multivision
5	Request to send	From Multivision
6	Data terminal ready	From Multivision
7	Ground	N/A
8	Carrier detect	From Multivision
20	Data set ready	To Multivision

*N/A, not applicable. N/C, not connected.

Company: Adds, Inc.
Product: Multivision Computer
Port: Serial   Pin Configuration: C01

Pin	Function	Direction
1	Ground	N/A
2	EIA out	From Multivision
3	EIA in	To Multivision
4	Request to send	From Multivision
5	Clear to send	To Multivision
6	Data set ready	To Multivision
7	Ground	N/A
8	Carrier detect	To Multivision
20	Data terminal ready	From Multivision

Company: Alphacom Inc.
Product: 20/40/84 Printers
Port: RS-232   Pin Configuration: P03

Pin	Function	Direction
2	Transmitted data	From printer
3	Received data	To printer
4	Request to send	From printer
5	Clear to send	To printer
6	Data set ready	To printer
7	Ground	N/A
20	Data terminal ready	From printer

Note: Pin 20 should be used for flow control.

Company: Alpha Microsystems
Product: AM-1000 Computer
Port: Serial   Pin Configuration: C03

Pin	Function	Direction
1	Chassis ground	N/A
2	Input data	To AM-1000
3	Output data	From Am-1000
4	Request to send	To AM-1000
5	Clear to send	From AM-1000
7	Signal ground	N/A
8	Rec. line signal detector	To Am-1000

Notes: (a) Pin 4 must be on before transmission can occur. Thus, the busy signal from a printer should be crossed to pin 4. (b) Pin 8 is toward the AM-1000.

Company: Altos Computer Systems
Product: ACS 8000 Computer
Port: A and B   Pin Configuration: C04

Pin	Function	Direction
1	Chassis ground	N/A
2	Transmitted data	From Altos
3	Received data	To Altos
4	Request to send	From Altos
5	Clear to send	To Altos
6	Data set ready	To Altos
7	Signal ground	N/A
20	Data terminal ready	To Altos

Notes: (a) Pin 8 is always high (on). (b) Pins 4 and 5 are not normally activated. (c) Pin 20 is an input signal used for flow control, a hardware XON/OFF capability.

Company: Amperex Electronic Corp.
Product: GP300 Printer
Port: RS-232   Pin Configuration: P03

Pin	Function	Direction
1	Protective ground	N/A
2	Transmitted data	From GP300
3	Received data	To GP300
4	Request to send	From GP300
5	Clear to send	To GP300
6	Data set ready	To GP300
7	Signal ground	N/A
8	Data carrier detect	To GP300
20	Data terminal ready	From GP300

Notes: (a) Pin 20 may be used for a busy indicator. (b) The GP300 also supports XON/XOFF and ACK/NAK sequences.

Company: Anacom General Corp.
Product: 150/160 Printers
Port: Serial   Pin Configuration: P04

Pin	Function	Direction
1	Chassis ground	N/A
3	Received data	To printer
4	Request to send	From printer
7	Signal ground	N/A
11	Printer busy	From printer
20	Data terminal ready	From printer
22	External power	To printer

Note: Pin 11 may be used for flow control.

Company: Anadex Inc.
Product: DP8000 and DP9000 Series Printers
Port: EIA (optioned for full-duplex)   Pin Configuration: P01

Pin	Function	Direction
1	Protective ground	N/A
2	Transmitted data	From DP8000
3	Received data	To DP8000
4	Request to send	From DP8000
5	Clear to send	To DP8000
6	Data set ready	To DP8000
7	Signal ground	N/A
8	Data carrier detect	To DP8000
19	Secondary request to send	From DP8000
20	Data terminal ready	From DP8000

Notes: (a) Pins 4 and 5 are internally jumpered, as are pins 6 and 8. (b) Pin 19 can be used for flow control. (c) A simplex mode of operation is possible using only pins 3, 7, and 19.

Company: Anderson Jacobson, Inc.
Product: AJ 510 CRT
Port: EIA Modem   Pin Configuration: T01

Pin	Function	Direction
1	Protective ground	N/A
2	Transmitted data	From AJ 510
3	Received data	To AJ 510
4	Request to send	From AJ 510
5	Clear to send	To AJ 510
6	Data set ready	To AJ 510
7	Signal ground	N/A
8	Carrier detect	To AJ 510
11	Secondary request to send	From AJ 510
12	Secondary carrier detect	To AJ 510
18	Modem remote test	N/A
19	Secondary request to send	From AJ 510
20	Data terminal ready	From AJ 510
24	Special internal clock	From AJ 510
25	Modem local test	N/A

Company: Anderson Jacobson, Inc.
Product: AJ 520 CRT
Port: Primary Communications Port   Pin Configuration: T01

Pin	Function	Direction
1	Protective ground	N/A
2	Transmitted data	From AJ 520
3	Received data	To AJ 520
4	Request to send	From AJ 520
5	Clear to send	To AJ 520
6	Data set ready	To AJ 520
7	Signal ground	N/A
8	Carrier detect	To AJ 520
9	Same as pin 18	
10	Same as pin 25	
11	Same as pin 19	
12	Secondary carrier detect	To AJ 520
15	Transmit clock	To AJ 520
17	Receive clock	To AJ 520
18	Modem remote test	N/A
19	Secondary request to send	From AJ 520
20	Data terminal ready	From AJ 520
22	Ring indicator	To AJ 520
25	Modem local test	N/A

Company: Anderson Jacobson, Inc.
Product: AJ 650 Ink Jet Printer
Port: RS-232-C   Pin Configuration: P05

Pin	Function	Direction
1	Protective ground	N/A
2	Transmitted data	From AJ 650
3	Received serial data	To AJ 650
4	Request to send	From AJ 650
5	Clear to send	To AJ 650
6	Data set ready	To AJ 650
7	Signal return	N/A
8	Data carrier detect	To AJ 650
11	Busy	From AJ 650
13	Alternate transmitted data	From AJ 650
14	Alternate busy	From AJ 650
15	Alternate data terminal ready	From AJ 650
20	Data terminal ready	From AJ 650

Notes: (a) Has software XON/XOFF transmit capability. (b) Pin 8 must be high for the printer to receive data. (c) Pin 11 can be used for hardware flow control.

Company: Anderson Jacobson, Inc.
Product: AJ 862 Printer Terminal
Port: EIA   Pin Configuration: P01

Pin	Function	Direction
1	Protective ground	N/A
2	Transmitted data	From AJ 862
3	Received data	To AJ 862
4	Request to send	From AJ 862
5	Clear to send	To AJ 862
7	Signal ground	N/A
8	Carrier detect	To AJ 862
11	Supervisory trans. data	From AJ 862
12	Supervisory rec. data	To AJ 862
14	Supervisory trans. data	From AJ 862
16	Supervisory rec. data	To AJ 862
19	Supervisory trans. data	From AJ 862
20	Data terminal ready	From AJ 862
25	Analog loopback/long func.	Special

Note: Pins 11, 12, 14, 16, and 19 are used in 202 mode only.

Company: Anderson Jacobson, Inc.
Product: AJ 880 Printer Terminal
Port: EIA Interface   Pin Configuration: P03

Pin	Function	Direction
1	Protective ground	N/A
2	Transmitted data	From AJ 880
3	Received data	To AJ 880
4	Request to send	From AJ 880
5	Clear to send	To AJ 880
6	Data set ready	To AJ 880
7	Signal ground	N/A
8	Carrier detect	To AJ 880
11	Secondary request to send	From AJ 880
12	Secondary carrier detect or speed indicator	To AJ 880
19	Secondary request to send	From AJ 880
20	Data terminal ready	From AJ 880
23	Speed select	From AJ 880

Note: Pin 20 (DTR) is dropped when any of these conditions is present: power is off, AJ 880 is in local, or a paper fault occurs.

Company: Ann Arbor Terminals, Inc.
Product: Ambassador Terminals
Port: Computer and Printer   Pin Configuration: T04

Pin	Function	Direction
2	Transmitted data	From Ambassador
3	Received data	To Ambassador
4	Request to send	From Ambassador
5	Clear to send	To Ambassador
7	Signal ground	N/A
20	Data terminal ready	From Ambassador

Note: The bottom port is generally for the computer, while the top port is for the printer.

Company: Apple Computer Inc.
Product: Apple III
Port: Port C   Pin Configuration: C01

Pin	Function	Direction
1	Protective ground	N/A
2	Transmitted data	From Apple III
3	Received data	To Apple III
4	Request to send	From Apple III
5	Clear to send	To Apple III
6	Data set ready	To Apple III
7	Signal ground	N/A
8	Data carrier detect	To Apple III
20	Data terminal ready	From Apple III

Notes: (a) If pin 6 is on, the Apple III assumes that the remote device is on and operational. (This could be used for hardware flow control.) (b) If pin 8 is on, the Apple III assumes that the remote device is ready to transmit data.

Company: Apple Computer Inc.
Product: Apple Communication Interface Card
Port: Serial   Pin Configuration: C05

Pin	Function	Direction
2	Transmitted data	From Comm. Card
3	Received data	To Comm. Card
4	Request to send	From Comm. Card
5	Clear to send	To Comm. Card
7	Signal ground	N/A

Notes: (a) Pins 6 and 20 are internally connected. (b) Pins 4 and 8 are internally connected.

Company: Apple Computer Inc.
Product: Serial Interface Card
Port: Serial   Pin Configuration: C06

Pin	Function	Direction
2	Received data	To serial card
3	Transmitted data	From serial card
7	Signal ground	N/A

Notes: (a) Pins 4 and 5 are internally wired together at the serial card. (b) Pins 6, 8, and 20 are jumpered together at the serial card.

Company: Apple Computer Inc.
Product: Super Serial Card
Port: Modem Position   Pin Configuration: C01

Pin	Function	Direction
1	Frame ground	N/A
2	Transmitted data	From SSC
3	Received data	To SSC
4	Request to send	From SSC
5	Clear to send	To SSC
6	Data set ready	To SSC
7	Signal ground	N/A
8	Data carrier detect	To SSC
19	Secondary clear to send	To SSC
20	Data terminal ready	From SSC

Note: The super serial card in this mode emulates data terminal equipment.

Company: Apple Computer Inc.
Product: Super Serial Card
Port: Terminal Position   Pin Configuration: C02

Pin	Function	Direction
1	Frame ground	N/A
2	Received data	To SSC
3	Transmitted data	From SSC
4	Request to send	To SSC
5	Clear to send	From SSC
6	Data set ready	From SSC
7	Signal ground	N/A
8	Data carrier detect	From SSC
20	Data terminal ready	To SSC

Note: This connection can be tricky if you fail to realize that in this mode the super serial card is emulating data communication equipment. It is internally jumpered to provide a null-modem cable function.

Company: Applied Digital Data Systems Inc.
Product: Regent 40 and 60
Port: EIA   Pin Configuration: T01

Pin	Function	Direction
1	Protective ground	N/A
2	Transmitted data	From Regent
3	Received data	To Regent
4	Request to send	From Regent
5	Clear to send	To Regent
6	Data set ready	To Regent
7	Signal ground	N/A
8	Rec. line signal detector	To Regent
11	Secondary request to send	From Regent
12	Secondary RLSD	To Regent
20	Data terminal ready	From Regent

Company: Applied Digital Data Systems Inc.
Product: Viewpoint CRT
Port: EIA   Pin Configuration: T04

Pin	Function	Direction
1	Protective ground	N/A
2	Transmitted data	From Viewpoint
3	Received data	To Viewpoint
4	Request to send	From Viewpoint
5	Clear to send	To Viewpoint
7	Signal ground	N/A
11	Secondary break indicator	From Viewpoint
20	Data terminal ready	From Viewpoint

Note: Supports up to 19,200 bps operation.

Company: Atari, Inc.
Product: Atari 400/800
Port: Port 1 on 850 Interface Module   Pin Configuration: C01

Pin	Function	Direction
1	Data terminal ready	From Atari
2	Data carrier detect	To Atari
3	Transmitted data	From Atari
4	Received data	To Atari
5	Signal ground	N/A
6	Data set ready	To Atari
7	Request to send	From Atari
8	Clear to send	To Atari

Note: These ports on the 850 interface modules are 9-pin connectors, not the standard DB-25 connector. I would suggest building a cable that converts them to a standard-size 25-pin connector prior to attempting to connect the Atari to other devices.

Company: Atari, Inc.
Product: Atari 400/800
Port: Ports 2 and 3 on 850 Interface Module   Pin Configuration: C07

Pin	Function	Direction
1	Data terminal ready	From Atari
3	Transmitted data	From Atari
4	Received data	To Atari
5	Signal ground	N/A
6	Data set ready	To Atari

Note: These ports are 9-pin female connectors. I would recommend converting them to a normal 25-pin connector prior to connecting peripherals to them.

Company: Atari, Inc.
Product: Atari 400/800
Port: Port 4 on 850 Interface Module   Pin Configuration: C08

Pin	Function	Direction
1	Data terminal ready	From Atari
3	Transmitted data	From Atari
4	Received data	To Atari
5	Signal ground	N/A
7	Request to send	From Atari

Note: This port is a 9-pin connector. I would recommend converting it to a standard 25-pin connector prior to connecting peripherals.

Company: Axiom Corp.
Product: EX-800 Printers
Port: HS Option   Pin Configuration: P06

Pin	Function	Direction
1	Protective ground	N/A
3	Received data	To printer
7	Circuit ground	N/A
20	Buffer overrun	From printer

Note: Without the HS option, the printers merely use the ground leads and pin 3 for input of data.

Company: Axiom Corp.
Product: IMP Printers
Port: HS Option   Pin Configuration: P05

Pin	Function	Direction
1	Chassis ground	N/A
2	Transmitted data	From printer
3	Received data	To printer
4	Request to send	From printer
6	Data set ready	To printer
7	Signal ground	N/A
8	Carrier detect	To printer
11	Busy	From printer
20	Off-line	From printer

Notes: (a) Two configurations are possible with the HS option: Configuration 1 is compatible with the standard Axiom; configuration 2 is compatible with the TI-810 printer. (b) Pins 6 and 8 must be on for the printer to receive data. (c) Pin 11 should be used for flow control.

Company: Axiom Corp.
Product: IMP Printers
Port: RS-232   Pin Configuration: P06

Pin	Function	Direction
1	Chassis ground	N/A
3	RS-232 input	To printer
7	Signal ground	N/A
20	Busy	From printer

Note: Option must be set to provide RS-232 as opposed to TTL levels on pin 20 before it may be used for busy signal.

Company: Beehive International
Product: DM 10/20/30, Basic (DM 5), Standard (DM 5A), Plus (DM 5B)
Port: Main   Pin Configuration: T01

Pin	Function	Direction
1	Protective ground	N/A
2	Transmitted data	From terminal
3	Received data	To terminal
4	Request to send	From terminal
5	Clear to send	To terminal
6	Data set ready	To terminal
7	Signal ground	N/A
20	Data terminal ready	From terminal

Note: If pin 5 is low, data transmission is prohibited. This can be used in flow control.

Company: Beehive International
Product: Topper Computer
Port: Auxiliary   Pin Configuration: C02

Pin	Function	Direction
1	Protective ground	N/A
2	Transmitted data	To Topper
3	Received data	From Topper
4	Request to send	To Topper
5	Clear to send	From Topper
6	Data set ready	From Topper
7	Signal ground	N/A
8	Data carrier detect	From Topper
20	Data terminal ready	To Topper

Note: If pin 20 is low, it indicates that the attached device is unable to receive data. This can be used for flow control.

Company: Beehive International
Product: Topper Computer
Port: Main   Pin Configuration: C01

Pin	Function	Direction
1	Protective ground	N/A
2	Transmitted data	From Topper
3	Received data	To Topper
4	Request to send	From Topper
5	Clear to send	To Topper
6	Data set ready	To Topper
7	Signal ground	N/A
20	Data terminal ready	From Topper

Note: If pin 5 is low, data transmission is prohibited. This can be used for flow control.

Company: Bell System
Product: Comm-Stor II
Port: Modem   Pin Configuration: C01

Pin	Function	Direction
1	Chassis ground	N/A
2	Transmitted data	From Comm-Stor
3	Received data	To Comm-Stor
4	Request to send	From Comm-Stor
5	Clear to send	To Comm-Stor
6	Data set ready	To Comm-Stor
7	Circuit ground	N/A
8	Carrier detect	To Comm-Stor
11	Secondary request to send	From Comm-Stor
12	Secondary carrier detect	To Comm-Stor
19	Secondary carrier detect	To Comm-Stor
20	Data terminal ready	From Comm-Stor
22	Ring indicator	To Comm-Stor

Company: Bell System
Product: Comm-Stor II
Port: Printer   Pin Configuration: C02

Pin	Function	Direction
1	Chassis ground	N/A
3	Received data	From Comm-Stor
6	Data set ready	From Comm-Stor
7	Circuit ground	N/A
8	Carrier detect	From Comm-Stor
11	Secondary request to send	To Comm-Stor
20	Data terminal ready	To Comm-Stor

Company: Bell System
Product: Comm-Stor II
Port: Terminal   Pin Configuration: C09

Pin	Function	Direction
1	Chassis ground	N/A
2	Transmitted data	To Comm-Stor
3	Received data	From Comm-Stor
4	Request to send	To Comm-Stor
5	Clear to send	From Comm-Stor
6	Data set ready	From Comm-Stor
7	Circuit ground	N/A
8	Carrier detect	From Comm-Stor
11	Secondary request to send	To Comm-Stor
12	Secondary carrier detect	From Comm-Stor
19	Secondary carrier detect	From Comm-Stor
20	Data terminal ready	To Comm-Stor
22	Ring indicator	From Comm-Stor

Company: Bell System
Product: DATASPEED 40 Printer
Port: RS-232   Pin Configuration: P05

Pin	Function	Direction
1	Protective ground	N/A
2	Transmitted data	From 40
3	Received data	To 40
4	Request to send	From 40
5	Clear to send	To 40
6	Data set ready	To 40
7	Signal ground	N/A
8	Data carrier detect	To 40
11	Supervisory transmitted data	From 40
12	Supervisory received data	To 40
20	Data terminal ready	From 40
22	Ring indicator	To 40
23	Alarm	N/A

Company: Bell System
Product: DATASPEED 40/2 Terminal
Port: COMM   Pin Configuration: T01

Pin	Function	Direction
1	Protective ground	N/A
2	Transmitted data	From 40/2
3	Received data	To 40/2
4	Request to send	From 40/2
5	Clear to send	To 40/2
6	Data set ready	To 40/2
7	Signal ground	N/A
8	Rec. line signal detector	To 40/2
11	Secondary request to send	From 40/2
19	Secondary request to send	From 40/2
20	Data terminal ready	From 40/2
22	Ring indicator	To 40/2

Note: If this port is optioned for full-duplex, pins 4, 11, and 19 are not present.

Company: Bell System
Product: DATASPEED 4420 Terminal
Port: Modem   Pin Configuration: T01

Pin	Function	Direction
1	Frame ground	N/A
2	Transmitted data	From 4420
3	Received data	To 4420
4	Request to send	From 4420
5	Clear to send	To 4420
6	Data set ready	To 4420
7	Signal ground	N/A
8	Rec. line signal detector	To 4420
11	Secondary request to send	From 4420
12	Secondary RLSD	To 4420
15	Transmission timing	To 4420
17	Receiver timing	To 4420
19	Secondary request to send	From 4420
20	Data terminal ready	From 4420
22	Ring indicator	To 4420

Note: Pins 15 and 17 are used with isochronous operation.

Company: Bell System
Product: Model 43 Teleprinter
Port: EIA   Pin Configuration: P03

Pin	Function	Direction
1	Protective ground	N/A
2	Transmitted data	From 43
3	Received data	To 43
4	Request to send	From 43
5	Clear to send	To 43
6	Data set ready	To 43
7	Signal ground	N/A
8	Carrier detect/RLSD	To 43
20	Data terminal ready	From 43
22	Ring indicator	To 43

Note: Pin 20 is affected by the paper supply.

Company: Bell System
Product: TP-1000 Teleprinter
Port: EIA   Pin Configuration: P01

Pin	Function	Direction
1	Protective ground	N/A
2	Transmitted data	From TP-1000
3	Received data	To TP-1000
4	Request to send	From TP-1000
5	Clear to send	To TP-1000
6	Data set ready	To TP-1000
7	Signal ground	N/A
8	Data carrier detect	To TP-1000
19	Secondary request to send	From TP-1000
20	Data terminal ready	From TP-1000
22	Ring indicator	To TP-1000

Note: Pin 19 can be used for flow control.

Company: Billings Computer Corporation
Product: 6000 Computer
Port: Serial   Pin Configuration: C09

Pin	Function	Direction
1	Protective ground	N/A
2	Transmitted data	To 6000
3	Received data	From 6000
4	Request to send	To 6000
5	Clear to send	From 6000
6	Data carrier detect	From 6000
7	Signal ground	N/A
15	Transmit clock	From 6000
17	Receive clock	From 6000
20	Data terminal ready	To 6000

Note: Either a two- or four-channel serial peripheral interface board is used to provide the ports.

Company: BMC
Product: IF800
Port: Serial   Pin Configuration: C09

Pin	Function	Direction
1	Protective ground	N/A
2	Received data	To IF800
3	Transmitted data	From IF800
4	Request to send	To IF800
5	Clear to send	From IF800
6	Data set ready	From IF800
7	Signal ground	N/A
8	Data carrier detect	From IF800
20	Data terminal ready	To IF800

Note: This port emulates data communication equipment.

Company: Burroughs Corp.
Product: B21 Computer
Port: RS-232(2)   Pin Configuration: C01

Pin	Function	Direction
1	Protective ground	N/A
2	Transmitted data	From B21
3	Received data	To B21
4	Request to send	From B21
5	Clear to send	To B21
6	Data set ready	To B21
7	Signal ground	N/A
8	Carrier detect	To B21
14	Secondary transmitted data	From B21
15	External transmit clock	To B21
16	Secondary received data	To B21
17	External receive clock	To B21
20	Data terminal ready	From B21
22	Ring indicator	To B21

Company: Burroughs Corp.
Product: B22 Computer
Port: A/B   Pin Configuration: C01

Pin	Function	Direction
1	Protective ground	N/A
2	Transmitted data	From B22
3	Received data	To B22
4	Request to send	From B22
5	Clear to send	To B22
6	Data set ready	To B22
7	Signal ground	N/A
8	Carrier detect	To B22
14	Secondary transmitted data	From B22
15	Transmit clock	To B22
16	Secondary received data	To B22
17	Receive clock	To B22
20	Data terminal ready	From B22
22	Ring indicator	To B22

Note: Port A may be configured as either an RS-232 or RS-422 port.

Company: California Computer Systems
Product: ASI-1, Model 7710A
Port: EIA   Pin Configuration: C09

Pin	Function	Direction
1	Protective ground	N/A
2	Transmitted data	To ASI
3	Received data	From ASI
4	Request to send	To ASI
5	Clear to send	From ASI
6	Data set ready	From ASI
7	Signal ground	N/A
8	Rec. line signal detector	From ASI
20	Data terminal ready	To ASI
24	Transmit clock (DTE)	To ASI

Note: Pins 6 and 8 are only passively supported.

Company: California Computer Systems
Product: Model 2719 S-100 Board
Port: Serial   Pin Configuration: C09

Pin	Function	Direction
1	Protective ground	N/A
2	Transmitted data	To 2719
3	Received data	From 2719
4	Request to send	To 2719
5	Clear to send	From 2719
6	Data set ready	From 2719
7	Signal ground	N/A
20	Data terminal ready	To 2719

Note: Emulates data communication equipment.

Company: Canon U.S.A., Inc.
Product: CX-1 and BX-3 Desk-Top Computers
Port: US1 and US2   Pin Configuration: C09

Pin	Function	Direction
1	Protective ground	N/A
2	Transmitted data	To computer
3	Received data	From computer
4	Request to send	To computer
5	Clear to send	From computer
6	Data set ready	From computer
7	Signal ground	N/A
8	Data carrier detect	From computer
20	Data terminal ready	To computer

Note: The ports are set up to emulate data communication equipment.

Company: Cardinal Scale Manufacturing Co.
Product: 2170 Printer
Port: Serial   Pin Configuration: P03

Pin	Function	Direction
1	Chassis ground	N/A
2	Transmitted data	From 2170
3	Received data	To 2170
4	Request to send	From 2170
5	Clear to send	To 2170
6	Data set ready	To 2170
7	Signal ground	N/A
8	Data carrier detect	To 2170
9	VCC	N/A
19	Signal ground	N/A
20	Data terminal ready	From 2170

Notes: (a) The printer can apply back pressure on pin 20. This is used for flow control. (b) Clear to send must be high. Manufacturer also recommends jumpering pins 8 to 9 and 7 to 19.

Company: Casio Inc.
Product: FX 9000P
Port: RS-232   Pin Configuration: P03

Pin	Function	Direction
1	Protective ground	N/A
2	Transmitted data	From Casio
3	Received data	To Casio
4	Request to send	From Casio
5	Clear to send	To Casio
6	Data set ready	To Casio
7	Signal ground	N/A
8	Data carrier detect	To Casio
20	Data terminal ready	From Casio
22	Ring indicator	To Casio

Notes: (a) A cable is connected to J3 to allow the 25-pin connector. (b) Either pin 4 or pin 20 can be used to indicate a busy signal.

Company: Centronics Data Computer Corporation
Product: 150 and 350 Series, 704-9, Adaptable Serial Interface
Port: Serial   Pin Configuration: P05

Pin	Function	Direction
1	Protective ground	N/A
2	Transmitted data	From printers
3	Received data	To printers
4	Request to send	From printers
5	Clear to send	To printers
6	Data set ready	To printers
7	Signal ground	N/A
8	Data carrier detect	To printers
11	Secondary request to send	From printers
20	Data terminal ready	From printers

Note: Pin 11 can be used for flow control.

Company: Centronics Data Computer Corporation
Product: 737-3 Printer
Port: RS-232   Pin Configuration: P07

Pin	Function	Direction
1	Protective ground	N/A
2	Transmitted data	From 737
3	Received data	To 737
6	Data set ready	To 737
7	Signal ground	N/A
8	Data carrier detect	To 737
11	Reverse channel	From 737
20	Data terminal ready	From 737

Notes: (a) Pins 6 and 8 must be on to allow data reception. (b) Pin 11 should be used for flow control.

Company: Centronics Data Compruter Corporation
Product: 761 Teleprinter
Port: RS-232   Pin Configuration: P05

Pin	Function	Direction
1	Protective ground	N/A
2	Transmitted data	From 761
3	Received data	To 761
4	Request to send	From 761
5	Clear to send	To 761
6	Data set ready	To 761
7	Signal ground	N/A
8	Data carrier detect	To 761
11	Transmit reverse channel	From 761
14	Transmit reverse channel	From 761
12	Receive reverse channel	To 761
16	Receive reverse channel	To 761
20	Data terminal ready	From 761
22	Ring indicator	To 761

Notes: (a) Pin 8 must be on for the printer to receive data. (b) Pin 11 or 14 may be used for flow control.

Company: Columbia Data Products, Inc.
Product: 1500/1800 Computers
Port: Serial (0–5)   Pin Configuration: C09

Pin	Function	Direction
2	Transmitted data	To computer
3	Received data	From computer
4	Request to send	To computer
5	Clear to send	From computer
6	Data set ready	From computer
7	Signal ground	N/A
15	Transmit clock	To computer
17	Receive clock	To computer
20	Data terminal ready	To computer
24	Internal transmit clock	From computer

Note: Pin 15 input is provided by pin 17 on ports 1, 3, and 5.

Company: Columbia Data Products, Inc.
Product: 1600 (MPC) Computer
Port: Console/Serial   Pin Configuration: C01

Pin	Function	Direction
1	Ground	N/A
2	Transmitted data	From MPC
3	Received data	To MPC
4	Request to send	From MPC
5	Clear to send	To MPC
6	Data set ready	To MPC
7	Ground	N/A
8	Data carrier detect	To MPC
20	Data terminal ready	From MPC
22	Ring indicator	To MPC

Company: Columbia Data Products, Inc.
Product: Commander F64 and 964 Computers
Port: Terminal (1, 2, and 3)   Pin Configuration: C09

Pin	Function	Direction
1	Protective ground	N/A
2	Transmitted data	To Commander
3	Received data	From Commander
4	Request to send	To Commander
5	Clear to send	From Commander
6	Data set ready	From Commander
7	Signal ground	N/A
8	Carrier detect	From Commander
20	Data terminal ready	To Commander

Note: These ports emulate DCE for direct connection to DTE devices.

Company: Columbia Data Products, Inc.
Product: Commander F64 and 964 Computers
Port: Modem (#4)   Pin Configuration: C01

Pin	Function	Direction
1	Protective ground	N/A
2	Transmitted data	From Commander
3	Received data	To Commander
4	Request to send	From Commander
5	Clear to send	To Commander
6	Data set ready	From Commander
7	Signal ground	N/A
8	Carrier detect	To Commander
12	Speed indicator	To Commander
15	Transmit clock	To Commander
17	Receive clock	To Commander
20	Data terminal ready	From Commander
22	Ring indicator	To Commander
23	Speed select	From Commander
24	Internal transmit clock	From Commander

Company: Columbia Data Products, Inc.
Product: Commander M64 Computer
Port: Modem/CPU   Pin Configuration: C01

Pin	Function	Direction
1	Protective ground	N/A
2	Transmitted data	From Commander
3	Received data	To Commander
4	Request to send	From Commander
5	Clear to send	To Commander
6	Data set ready	To Commander
7	Signal ground	N/A
20	Data terminal ready	From Commander
22	Ring indicator	To Commander

Company: Columbia Data Products, Inc.
Product: Commander M64 Computer
Port: Terminal   Pin Configuration: C09

Pin	Function	Direction
1	Protective ground	N/A
2	Transmitted data	To Commander
3	Received data	From Commander
4	Request to send	To Commander
5	Clear to send	From Commander
6	Data set ready	From Commander
7	Signal ground	N/A
8	Carrier detect	From Commander
20	Data terminal ready	To Commander

Company: Columbia Data Products, Inc.
Product: Concept 1000/DC Computers
Port: Console and Auxiliary   Pin Configuration: C09

Pin	Function	Direction
1	Protective ground	N/A
2	Transmitted data	To Commander
3	Received data	From Commander
4	Request to send	To Commander
5	Clear to send	From Commander
6	Data set ready	From Commander
7	Signal ground	N/A
8	Carrier detect	From Commander
20	Data terminal ready	To Commander

Note: Pins 6 and 8 are internally tied together.

Company: Columbia Data Products, Inc.
Product: Concept 1000/DC-1000 Computers
Port: Modem   Pin Configuration: C01

Pin	Function	Direction
1	Protective ground	N/A
2	Transmitted data	From computer
3	Received data	To computer
4	Request to send	From computer
5	Clear to send	To computer
6	Data set ready	From computer
7	Signal ground	N/A
8	Carrier detect	To computer
15	Transmit clock	To computer
17	Receive clock	To computer
20	Data terminal ready	From computer

Company: Commodore Business Machines
Product: Super PET (9000 Series) Computer
Port: Serial   Pin Configuration: C01

Pin	Function	Direction
1	Protective ground	N/A
2	Transmitted data	From PET
3	Received data	To PET
4	Request to send	From PET
5	Clear to send	To PET
6	Data set ready	To PET
7	Signal ground	N/A
8	Carrier detect	To PET
20	Data terminal ready	From PET

Company: Commodore Business Machines
Product: VIC-20
Port: RS-232   Pin Configuration: C01

Pin	Function	Direction
1	Protective ground	N/A
2	Transmitted data	From VIC-20
3	Received data	To VIC-20
4	Request to send	From VIC-20
5	Clear to send	To VIC-20
6	Data set ready	To VIC-20
7	Signal ground	N/A
8	Rec. line signal detector	To VIC-20
20	Data terminal ready	From VIC-20
22	Ring indicator	To VIC-20

Company: Comrex International Inc.
Product: Comriter Printer
Port: RS-232-C   Pin Configuration: P05

Pin	Function	Direction
1	Frame ground	N/A
2	Transmitted data	From Comriter
3	Received data	To Comriter
4	Request to send	From Comriter
5	Clear to send	To Comriter
6	Data set ready	To Comriter
7	Signal ground	N/A
8	Rec. line signal detector	To Comriter
11	Reverse channel	From Comriter
20	Data terminal ready	From Comriter

Notes: (a) Pins 5, 6, and 8 must be on before data can be transmitted. (b) Pin 4 is high when printer has power. (c) Pin 11 or pin 20 may be used for printer status. (d) The Comriter also supports XON/XOFF control characters.

Company: Convergent Technologies
Product: 1000 Computer
Port: Serial   Pin Configuration: C01

Pin	Function	Direction
1	Protective ground	N/A
2	Transmitted data	From 1000
3	Received data	To 1000
4	Request to send	From 1000
5	Clear to send	To 1000
6	Data set ready	To 1000
7	Signal ground	N/A
8	Carrier detect	To 1000
14	Secondary transmitted data	From 1000
15	Transmit clock	To 1000
16	Secondary received data	To 1000
17	Receive clock	To 1000
20	Data terminal ready	From 1000
22	Ring indicator	To 1000

Company: Corvus Systems
Product: Concept Computer
Port: RS-232 Port 1   Pin Configuration: C01

Pin	Function	Direction
1	Chassis ground	N/A
2	Transmitted data	From Concept
3	Received data	To Concept
4	Request to send	From Concept
5	Clear to send	To Concept
6	Data set ready	To Concept
7	Signal ground	N/A
8	Data carrier detect	To Concept
20	Data terminal ready	From Concept

Company: Corvus Systems
Product: Concept Computer
Port: Serial Printer 0   Pin Configuration: C01

Pin	Function	Direction
1	Chassis ground	N/A
2	Transmitted data	From Concept
3	Received data	To Concept
4	Request to send	From Concept
5	Clear to send	To Concept
6	Data set ready	To Concept
7	Signal ground	N/A
8	Data carrier detect	To Concept
20	Data terminal ready	From Concept

Company: Cromemco, Inc.
Product: Quadart
Port: J3, J5, J7, and J9   Pin Configuration: C01

Pin	Function	Direction
2	Transmitted data	From Quadart
3	Received data	To Quadart
4	Request to send	From Quadart
5	Clear to send	To Quadart
6	Data set ready	To Quadart
7	Signal ground	N/A
8	Data carrier detect	To Quadart
11	CY	From Quadart
15	Transmit clock	To Quadart
17	Receive clock	To Quadart
20	Data terminal ready	From Quadart
22	Ring indicator	To Quadart
24	External clock	From Quadart

Note: Consult instruction manual for function of pin 11.

Company: Cromemco, Inc.
Product: Tu-Art Digital Interface
Port: J4 Serial A and J5 Serial B   Pin Configuration: C10

Pin	Function	Direction
1	Frame ground	N/A
2	Input A/B	To Tu-Art
3	Output A/B	From Tu-Art
6	Data set ready	From Tu-Art
7	Signal ground	N/A
8	Clear to send	From Tu-Art

Note: Pins 2 and 3 are transmitted and received data, respectively. These two ports are set up to emulate DCE.

Company: Data General Corporation
Product: Dasher D100/200 and G300 Display Terminals
Port: EIA   Pin Configuration: T01

Pin	Function	Direction
2	Transmitted data	From terminals
3	Received data	To terminals
4	Request to send	From terminals
5	Clear to send	To terminals
6	Data set ready	To terminals
7	Signal ground	N/A
8	Data carrier detect	To terminals
20	Data terminal ready	From terminals

Note: If pin 5 is off, the terminal cannot transmit data.

Company: Data General Corporation
Product: Dasher TP1 Terminal Printer
Port: EIA   Pin Configuration: P08

Pin	Function	Direction
2	Transmitted data	From TP1
3	Received data	To TP1
7	Signal ground	N/A
20	Data terminal ready	From TP1

Note: Pin 20 controls the printer busy status and can be used for flow control.

Company: Data General Corporation
Product: Dasher TP2 Printer
Port: Serial   Pin Configuration: P08

Pin	Function	Direction
2	Transmitted data	From TP2
3	Received data	To TP2
4	Request to send	From TP2
5	Clear to send	To TP2
6	Data set ready	To TP2
7	Signal ground	N/A
20	Data terminal ready	From TP2

Note: Pin 4 is held tight as long as data can be received. Should the buffer begin to fill up, this lead will go low. This can be used for hardware flow control; however, software XON/XOFF can be used.

Company: Data General Corporation
Product: MPT/100 Computer
Port: Communication/Printer   Pin Configuration: C01

Pin	Function	Direction
2	Transmitted data	From MPT/100
3	Received data	To MPT/100
4	Request to send	From MPT/100
5	Clear to send	To MPT/100
6	Data set ready	To MPT/100
7	Signal ground	N/A
8	Data carrier detect	To MPT/100
15	Transmit clock	To MPT/100
17	Receive clock	To MPT/100
20	Data terminal ready	From MPT/100
24	Transmit clock	From MPT/100

Note: Both ports are the same, although labeled differently.

Company: Data Impact Printer, Inc.
Product: DIP-85 Printer
Port: RS-232   Pin Configuration: P08

Pin	Function	Direction
1	Chassis ground	N/A
2	Transmitted data	From DIP-85
3	Received data	To DIP-85
5	Clear to send	From DIP-85
7	Signal ground	N/A
20	Data terminal ready	From DIP-85

Notes: (a) Pins 5 and 20 may be used for busy indicator. (b) The DIP-85 supports XON/XOFF characters.

Company: Datamac Computer Systems
Product: 800/1600 Computers
Port: A   Pin Configuration: C01

Pin	Function	Direction
1	Chassis ground	N/A
2	Transmitted data	From 800
3	Received data	To 800
4	Request to send	From 800
5	Clear to send	To 800
6	Data set ready	To 800
7	Logic ground	N/A
8	Data carrier detect	To 800
20	Data terminal ready	From 800

Note: This port is for a modem connection.

Company: Datamac Computer Systems
Product: 800/1600 Computers
Port: B   Pin Configuration: C09

Pin	Function	Direction
1	Chassis ground	N/A
2	Transmitted data	To 800
3	Received data	From 800
5	Clear to send	From 800
6	Data set ready	From 800
7	Logic ground	N/A
8	Data carrier detect	From 800
12	Secondary data carrier detect	From 800
13	Secondary clear to send	From 800
14	Secondary transmitted data	To 800
15	Transmission signal timing	From 800
16	Secondary received data	From 800
17	Receive signal timing	From 800
19	Secondary request to send	To 800
20	Data terminal ready	To 800
22	Ring indicator	From 800
24	Transmit signal timing	To 800

Note: This port is configured for direct connection to a printer.

Company: Datamac Computer Systems
Product: Async Adaptor Board
Port: 1/2   Pin Configuration: C01

Pin	Function	Direction
1	Chassis ground	N/A
2	Transmitted data	From AAB
3	Received data	To AAB
4	Request to send	From AAB
5	Clear to send	To AAB
6	Data set ready	To AAB
7	Logic ground	N/A
8	Carrier detect	To AAB
20	Data terminal ready	From AAB
22	Ring indicator	To AAB

Note: A shunt plug is available for configuration as either DTE or DCE.

Company: Dataproducts Corp.
Product: M-100 Printer
Port: Serial   Pin Configuration: P01

Pin	Function	Direction
1	Protective ground	N/A
2	Transmitted data	From printer
3	Received data	To printer
4	Request to send	From printer
5	Clear to send	To printer
6	Data set ready	To printer
7	Signal ground	N/A
8	Rec. line signal detector	To printer
11	Busy	From printer
19	Busy	From printer
20	Data terminal ready	From printer
22	Ring indicator	To printer

Notes: (a) Either pin 11 or pin 19 may be used for flow control. (b) Pins 4, 5, 6, and 20 must be on before the printer can transmit data. (c) Pin 20 and, optionally, pins 6 and 8 must be on for the printer to receive data.

Company: DATASOUTH Computer Corp.
Product: DS 180 Printer
Port: RS-232   Pin Configuration: P07

Pin	Function	Direction
1	Chassis ground	N/A
2	Serial data out	From DS 180
3	Serial data in	To DS 180
7	Signal ground	N/A
8	Carrier detect	To DS 180
11	Data terminal ready	From DS 180
20	Data terminal ready	From DS 180

Notes: (a) Either pin 11 or pin 20 may be used for busy indicator. (b) The DS 180 does support XON/XOFF protocol.

Company: Datavue Corporation
Product: 100, 200, 300 Series Displaymaster CRTs
Port: Communications Port   Pin Configuration: T01

Pin	Function	Direction
1	Chassis ground	N/A
2	Transmitted data	From CRT
3	Received data	To CRT
4	Request to send	From CRT
5	Clear to send	To CRT
6	Data set ready	To CRT
7	Signal and logic ground	N/A
20	Data terminal ready	From CRT

Note: Optionally, pins 15 and 17 can be transmit and receive clocks, respectively, for synchronous operation.

Company: Datavue Corporation
Product: DV-80 Computer
Port: CRT Terminal and Auxiliary Ports   Pin Configuration: C09

Pin	Function	Direction
1	Frame ground	N/A
2	Transmitted data	To DC-80
3	Received data	From DV-80
4	Request to send	To DV-80
5	Clear to send	From DV-80
7	Signal ground	N/A
20	Data terminal ready	To DV-80

Company: Diablo Systems, Inc.
Product: Model 1610/1620 Printers
Port: EIA   Pin Configuration: P03

Pin	Function	Direction
1	Protective ground	N/A
2	Transmitted data	From printers
3	Received data	To printers
4	Request to send	From printers
5	Clear to send	To printers
6	Data set ready	To printers
7	Signal ground	N/A
8	Rec. line signal detector	To printers
20	Data terminal ready	From printers
23	Data signal rate selector	N/C

Notes: (a) Pin 23 is included for possible future use. (b) These printers support the ETX/ACK protocol and should be used when operating at 1200 bps to prevent overflow.

Company: Diablo Systems, Inc.
Product: KSR 1640/1650
Port: EIA   Pin Configuration: P03

Pin	Function	Direction
1	Protective ground	N/A
2	Transmitted data	From printers
3	Received data	To printers
4	Request to send	From printers
5	Clear to send	To printers
6	Data set ready	To printers
7	Signal ground	N/A
8	Rec. line signal detector	To printers
20	Data terminal ready	From printers

Notes: (a) Pin 4 is always high. (b) Pin 6 must be high to receive data. (c) Pin 5 must be high to transmit data. (d) Pin 20 can provide flow control.

Company: Diablo Systems, Inc.
Product: Model 620
Port: Serial   Pin Configuration: P03

Pin	Function	Direction
2	Transmitted data	From 620
3	Received data	To 620
4	Request to send	From 620
6	Data set ready	To 620
7	Signal ground	N/A
20	Data terminal ready	From 620

Notes: (a) Pin 4 is always high. (b) Pin 6 must be on to before data can be received. (c) Flow control is switch-selectable. (d) Pin 20 is used for the hardware XON/XOFF function.

Company: Diablo Systems, Inc.
Product: RO 630
Port: EIA   Pin Configuration: P05

Pin	Function	Direction
1	Protective ground	N/A
2	Transmitted data	From 630
3	Received data	To 630
4	Request to send	From 630
5	Clear to send	To 630
6	Data set ready	To 630
7	Signal ground	N/A
8	Rec. line signal detector	To 630
11	Printer ready	From 630
20	Data terminal ready	From 630

Notes: (a) Pin 4 is always high. (b) Pin 6 must be on before 630 can receive data. (c) Pin 20 can be used for hardware flow control instead of pin 11.

Company: Digital Equipment Corp.
Product: LA Series Printers
Port: EIA   Pin Configuration: P01

Pin	Function	Direction
1	Frame ground	N/A
2	Transmitted data	From printer
3	Received data	To printer
4	Request to send	From printer
5	Clear to send	To printer
6	Data set ready	To printer
7	Signal ground	N/A
8	Data carrier detect	To printer
11	Secondary request to send	From printer
12	Speed indicator/SDCD	To printer
19	Secondary request to send	From printer
20	Data terminal ready	From printer
22	Ring indicator	To printer
23	Speed select	From printer

Note: Either pin 11 or pin 19 may be used for hardware flow control, although software XON/XOFF capability exists.

Company: Digital Equipment Corp.
Product: Rainbow PC-100
Port: Communication   Pin Configuration: C01

Pin	Function	Direction
1	Protective ground	N/A
2	Transmitted data	From PC-100
3	Received data	To PC-100
4	Request to send	From PC-100
5	Clear to send	To PC-100
6	Data set ready	To PC-100
7	Signal ground	N/A
8	Carrier detect	To PC-100
15	Transmit clock	To PC-100
17	Receive clock	To PC-100
19	Secondary request to send	From PC-100
20	Data terminal ready	From PC-100
22	Ring indicator	To PC-100
23	Speed select	From PC-100

Company: Digital Equipment Corp.
Product: Rainbow PC-100
Port: Printer   Pin Configuration: C02

Pin	Function	Direction
1	Protective ground	N/A
2	Transmitted data	To PC-100
3	Received data	From PC-100
5	Clear to send	From PC-100
6	Data set ready	From PC-100
7	Signal ground	N/A
20	Data terminal ready	To PC-100

Note: Pins 5 and 6 are always asserted.

Company: Digital Equipment Corp.
Product: VT-100 Series Terminals
Port: Communication   Pin Configuration: T01

Pin	Function	Direction
1	Protective ground	N/A
2	Transmitted data	From VT-100
3	Received data	To VT-100
4	Request to send	From VT-100
5	Clear to send	To VT-100
6	Data set ready	To VT-100
7	Signal ground	N/A
8	Carrier detect	To VT-100
11	Secondary request to send	From VT-100
12	Secondary carrier detect	To VT-100
15	Transmit clock	To VT-100
17	Receive clock	To VT-100
19	Secondary request to send	From VT-100
20	Data terminal ready	From VT-100
22	Ring indicator	To VT-100
23	Secondary request to send	From VT-100

Notes: (a) Pins 5, 6, 8, 15, 17, and 22 are ignored at all times by the basic VT-100 terminals. (b) Pins 11, 19, and 23 may also be used for a speed select signal from the VT-100. (c) Pin 4 is asserted at all times when the VT-100 is on.

Company: DTC Inc.
Product: Micro 210 Computer
Port: DCL (1–3)   Pin Configuration: C01

Pin	Function	Direction
1	Earth ground	N/A
2	Data out	From 210
3	Data in	To 210
4	Request to send	From 210
5	Clear to send	To 210
6	Data set ready	To 210
7	Signal ground	N/A
20	Data terminal ready	From 210

Company: DTC Inc.
Product: Micro 210 Computer
Port: DTE (0)   Pin Configuration: C09

Pin	Function	Direction
1	Earth ground	N/A
2	Data in	To 210
3	Data out	From 210
4	Request to send	To 210
5	Clear to send	From 210
6	Data set ready	From 210
7	Signal ground	N/A
20	Data terminal ready	To 210

Note: Pin 4 must be true (positive) before the 210 will transmit.

Company: Dual Systems Corp.
Product: System 83 Computer
Port: Serial   Pin Configuration: C09

Pin	Function	Direction
2	Transmitted data	To System 83
3	Received data	From System 83
4	Request to send	To System 83
5	Clear to send	From System 83
6	Data set ready	From System 83
7	Signal ground	N/A
8	Rec. line signal detector	From System 83
17	Receive signal timing	From System 83
20	Data terminal ready	To System 83
24	Transmit signal timing	To System 83

Notes: (a) This RS-232 interface is provided by the SIO-4/DMA serial I/O board. Four ports are provided by this board. The standard configuration of each port is for direct connection to a terminal or printer; however, options are available for connection to a modem. (b) XON/XOFF and ETX/ACK are supported by the board. (c) Pin 20 may be used for hardware flow control.

Company: Dynabyte
Product: Dynabyte 5000 Computer
Port: CPU1 and CPU2   Pin Configuration: C13

Pin	Function	Direction
2	Data in	To 5000
3	Data out	From 5000
5	Terminal ready	To 5000
7	Ground	N/A

Notes: Pin 5 must be on to transmit data.

Company: Eagle Computer, Inc.
Product: Eagle I, II, III, IV, and V
Port: Serial   Pin Configuration: C15

Pin	Function	Direction
2	Received data	To Eagle
3	Transmitted data	From Eagle
4	Request to send	From Eagle
5	Clear to send/printer busy	To Eagle
7	Ground	N/A

Note: Hardware flow control is accomplished by using pin 5.

Company: Epson America, Inc.
Product: MX-70/80/100 Series
Port: RS-232-C   Pin Configuration: P07

Pin	Function	Direction
1	Protective ground	N/A
2	Transmitted data	From MX
3	Received data	To MX
6	Data set ready	To MX
7	Signal ground	N/A
8	Data carrier detect	To MX
11	Reverse channel	From MX
20	Data terminal ready	From MX

Notes: (a) Pin 6 must be on for the printer to receive data. (b) Pin 8 is the same signal as pin 6. (c) Pin 11 can be used for flow control.

Company: Epson America, Inc.
Product: MX-20 Series
Port: RS-232   Pin Configuration: C01

Pin	Function	Direction
1	Case ground	N/A
2	Transmitted data	From MX-20
3	Received data	To MX-20
4	Request to send	From MX-20
5	Clear to send	To MX-20
6	Data set ready	To MX-20
7	Signal ground	N/A
8	Carrier detect	To MX-20
20	Data terminal ready	From MX-20

Note: This configuration assumes that a cable has been attached that converts the eight-pin DIN connector to an RS-232-compatible-size plug.

Company: Extel Corporation
Product: B318 Series
Port: RS-232   Pin Configuration: P10

Pin	Function	Direction
1	Protective ground	N/A
2	Transmitted data	From Extel
3	Received data	To Extel
4	Request to send	From Extel
5	Clear to send	To Extel
6	Data set ready	To Extel
7	Signal ground	N/A
8	Data carrier detect	To Extel
20	Data terminal ready	From Extel

Note: Loss of pin 6 restricts data transmission.

Company: Facit, Inc.
Product: 4500 Series Printer
Port: RS-232   Pin Configuration: P03

Pin	Function	Direction
1	Protective ground	N/A
2	Transmitted data	From printer
3	Received data	To printer
4	Request to send	From printer
5	Clear to send	To printer
6	Data set ready	To printer
7	Signal ground	N/A
8	Rec. line signal detector	To printer
15	Transmit timing	To printer
17	Receive timing	To printer
20	Data terminal ready	From printer

Notes: (a) Pin 20 may be optioned for flow control. (b) The printers support XON/XOFF characters.

Company: Florida Data Corp.
Product: OSP100 Series Printer
Port: Serial   Pin Configuration: P05

Pin	Function	Direction
1	Frame ground	N/A
2	Transmitted data	From printer
3	Received data	To printer
4	Request to send	From printer
5	Clear to send	To printer
6	Data set ready	To printer
7	Signal ground	N/A
11	Ready	From printer
20	Data terminal ready	From printer

Notes: (a) XON/XOFF and ETX/ACK protocols are supported. (b) Pin 11 or pin 20 may be used for hardware flow control. (c) Pin 6 must be on for data reception to occur. (d) Pin 5 must be on for data transmission to occur.

Company: Fujitsu America, Inc.
Product: SP830 Character Printer
Port: Serial   Pin Configuration: P03

Pin	Function	Direction
1	Protective ground	N/A
2	Transmitted data	From SP830
3	Received data	To SP830
4	Request to send	From SP830
5	Clear to send	To SP830
6	Data set ready	To SP830
7	Signal ground	N/A
8	Data carrier detect	To SP830
20	Data terminal ready	From SP830

Note: Either pin 20 or pin 11 may be used for hardware flow control, although software XON/XOFF capability can be used.

Company: General Electric Company
Product: GE 2120 Printer
Port: EIA   Pin Configuration: P03

Pin	Function	Direction
1	Protective ground	N/A
2	Transmitted data	From 2120
3	Received data	To 2120
4	Request to send	From 2120
5	Clear to send	To 2120
6	Data set ready	To 2120
7	Signal ground	N/A
8	Rec. line signal detector	To 2120
11	Secondary request to send	From 2120
12	Secondary RLSD (202)	To 2120
12	Speed indicator (212)	To 2120
19	Secondary request to send	From 2120
20	Data terminal ready	From 2120
22	Ring indicator	To 2120
23	Speed selector (212)	From 2120

Notes: (a) The function of pin 12 depends on the environment of either a 202 or 212 modem configuration. (b) XON/XOFF is supported; pin 20 is also optionable for hardware flow control.

Company: General Electric Company
Product: 2030 Printer
Port: EIA   Pin Configuration: P03

Pin	Function	Direction
1	Protective ground	N/A
2	Transmitted data	From 2030
3	Received data	To 2030
4	Request to send	From 2030
5	Clear to send	To 2030
6	Data set ready	To 2030
7	Signal ground	N/A
8	Rec. line signal detector	To 2030
20	Data terminal ready	From 2030
22	Ring indicator	To 2030

Notes: XON/XOFF is supported; pin 20 is also optionable for hardware flow control.

Company: General Electric Company
Product: TermiNet 300 Printer
Port: Modem   Pin Configuration: P03

Pin	Function	Direction
1	Protective ground	N/A
2	Transmitted data	From 300
3	Received data	To 300
5	Clear to send	To 300
6	Data set ready	To 300
7	Signal ground	N/A
8	Rec. line signal detector	To 300
20	Data terminal ready	From 300
22	Ring indicator	To 300

Company: Gnat Computers Inc.
Product: System 10 Computer
Port: Modem   Pin Configuration: C01

Pin	Function	Direction
2	Serial out	From computer
3	Serial in	To computer
4	Request to send	From computer
5	Clear to send	To computer
6	Data set ready	To computer
7	Signal ground	N/A
8	Data carrier detect	To computer
20	Data terminal ready	From computer

Note: XON/XOFF is supported.

Company: Gnat Computers Inc.
Product: System 10 Computer
Port: Terminal   Pin Configuration: C09

Pin	Function	Direction
2	Serial in	To computer
3	Serial out	From computer
4	Data carrier detect	To computer
5	Data terminal ready	From computer
6	Data terminal ready	From computer
7	Signal ground	N/A
8	Request to send	From computer
20	Data set ready/clear to send	To computer

Notes: (a) The terminal port is designed as a null modem. Direct connection of a terminal is allowed as a result of this configuration. (b) The Gnat computers are supported by Digital Technology International.

Company: Gulton Industries, Inc.
Product: AP-20 Printer
Port: Serial (TAC314-A)   Pin Configuration: P11

Pin	Function	Direction
1	Protective ground	N/A
3	Received data	To printer
6	Data set ready	To printer
7	Signal ground	N/A
20	Data terminal ready	From printer

Note: Pin 20 should be used for hardware flow control.

Company: Hazeltine Corporation
Product: 1400, 1500, Esprit I and II, and Executive Series CRTs
Port: EIA   Pin Configuration: T01

Pin	Function	Direction
1	Protective ground	N/A
2	Transmitted data	From CRT
3	Received data	To CRT
4	Request to send	From CRT
5	Clear to send	To CRT
6	Data set ready	To CRT
7	Signal ground	N/A
8	Data carrier detect	To CRT
20	Data terminal ready	From CRT

Note: Certain models of the Esprit and Executive series offer a bidirectional auxiliary port.

Company: Heath Company
Product: H-8 Computer
Port: DCE   Pin Configuration: C01

Pin	Function	Direction
1	Protective ground	N/A
2	DCE input	From H-8
3	DCE output	To H-8
4	Request to send	From H-8
5	Clear to send	To H-8
6	Data set ready	To H-8
7	Signal ground	N/A
8	Rec. line signal detector	To H-8
20	Data terminal ready	From H-8

Notes: (a) A cable is not supplied with this port. (b) This port is configured to connect to a modem.

Company: Heath Company
Product: H-8 Computer
Port: DTE   Pin Configuration: C09

Pin	Function	Direction
1	Protective ground	N/A
2	DTE output	To H-8
3	DTE input	From H-8
4	Request to send	To H-8
5	Clear to send	From H-8
6	Data set ready	From H-8
7	Signal ground	N/A
8	Rec. line signal detector	From H-8
20	Data terminal ready	To H-8

Note: These labels apply to the WH8-41 cable that is supplied.

Company: Heath Company
Product: H-8 Computer
Port: Serial (H8-4)   Pin Configuration: C09

Pin	Function	Direction
1	Protective ground	N/A
2	DTE output	To H-8
3	DTE input	From H-8
4	Request to send	To H-8
5	Clear to send	From H-8
6	Data set ready	From H-8
7	Signal ground	N/A
8	Rec. line signal detector	From H-8
20	Data terminal ready	To H-8

Notes: (a) This port is provided by the WH8-41 cable (supplied). (b) Ports 0–3 are all the same.

Company: Heath Company
Product: A-14 Computer
Port: Serial   Pin Configuration: P09

Pin	Function	Direction
1	Protective ground	N/A
2	Serial output	From printer
3	Serial input	To printer
4	Request to send	From printer
6	Data set ready	To printer
7	Signal ground	N/A
15	Print not busy	From printer
20	Data terminal ready	From printer

Notes: (a) Pin 4 should be used for flow control. (b) Pins 6 and 15 are not required for operation.

Company: Heath Company
Product: H-25 Printer
Port: Serial   Pin Configuration: P12

Pin	Function	Direction
1	Protective ground	N/A
2	Serial output	From printer
3	Serial input	To printer
4	Busy	From printer
7	Signal common	N/A

Notes: (a) Pin 4 is used for flow control. (b) The cable supplied with the printer connects pins 1–7, 11, and 20 straight through.

Company: Heath Company
Product: H-89A and H-88(A) Computers
Port: DTE   Pin Configuration: C01

Pin	Function	Direction
1	Protective ground	N/A
2	Transmitted data	From H-89
3	Received data	To H-89
4	Request to send	From H-89
5	Clear to send	To H-89
6	Data set ready	To H-89
7	Signal ground	N/A
8	Rec. line signal detector	To H-89
20	Data terminal ready	From H-89

Notes: (a) Cable 134–1070 is connected to plug P605 to give this port. (b) The model HA-88-3 serial interface allows this port for the H-88(A) computers.

Company: Heath Company
Product: H-89 Computer
Port: DTE (330/337)   Pin Configuration: C01

Pin	Function	Direction
1	Protective ground	N/A
2	Transmitted data	From H-89
3	Received data	To H-89
4	Request to send	From H-89
5	Clear to send	To H-89
6	Data set ready	To H-89
7	Signal ground	N/A
8	Rec. line signal detector	To H-89
20	Data terminal ready	From H-89

Note: The DTE port is set up to connect to a modem.

Company: Heath Company
Product: H-89 Computer
Port: Printer and DCE Ports   Pin Configuration: C09

Pin	Function	Direction
1	Protective ground	N/A
2	Transmitted data	To H-89
3	Received data	From H-89
4	Request to send	To H-89
5	Clear to send	From H-89
6	Data set ready	From H-89
7	Signal ground	N/A
8	Rec. line signal detector	From H-89
20	Data terminal ready	To H-89

Notes: (a) The printer port (340/347) is a line printer port. (b) The DCE port is port 320/327.

Company: Heath Company
Product: H-89A and H-88(A) Computers
Port: Line Printer and DCE   Pin Configuration: C09

Pin	Function	Direction
1	Protective ground	N/A
2	Transmitted data	To H-89
3	Received data	From H-89
4	Request to send	To H-89
5	Clear to send	From H-89
6	Data set ready	From H-89
7	Signal ground	N/A
8	Rec. line signal detector	From H-89
20	Data terminal ready	To H-89

Notes: (a) Cable 134–1073 is connected to plugs P603/P604 to give these ports. (b) The model HA-88-3 serial interface provides the se ports for the HA-88(A) computers.

Company: Hewlett-Packard
Product: HP125 Computer
Port: 2   Pin Configuration: C01

Pin	Function	Direction
1	Shield	N/A
2	Transmitted data	From HP125
3	Received data	To HP125
4	Request to send	From HP125
5	Clear to send	To HP125
6	Data mode	To HP125
7	Signal ground	N/A
8	Receive ready	To HP125
20	Data terminal ready	From HP125

Company: Hewlett-Packard
Product: Series 80 Personal Computers
Port: 82939 Option 001 Cable   Pin Configuration: C01

Pin	Function	Direction
1	Protective ground	N/A
2	Transmitted data	From computer
3	Received data	To computer
4	Request to send	From computer
5	Clear to send	To computer
6	Data set ready	To computer
7	Signal ground	N/A
8	Carrier detect	To computer
20	Data terminal ready	From computer
23	Data rate select	From computer

Company: Hewlett-Packard
Product: Series 80 Personal Computers
Port: 82939 Standard Cable   Pin Configuration: C09

Pin	Function	Direction
1	Protective ground	N/A
2	Transmitted data	To computer
3	Received data	From computer
4	Request to send	To computer
5	Clear to send	From computer
6	Data set ready	From computer
7	Signal ground	N/A
8	Carrier detect	From computer
20	Data terminal ready	To computer
23	Data rate select	To computer

Company: HI-G Co., Inc.
Product: 9/80 and 9/132 Printers
Port: RS-232   Pin Configuration: P04

Pin	Function	Direction
1	Frame ground	N/A
2	Transmitted data	From printer
3	Received data	To printer
4	Request to send	From printer
7	Signal ground	N/A
11	Auxiliary busy	From printer
20	Data terminal ready	From printer

Note: Pin 11 should be used for flow control.

Company: IBM
Product: 3101 Display Terminal
Port: Communication Interface   Pin Configuration: T01

Pin	Function	Direction
1	Frame ground	N/A
2	Transmitted data	From 3101
3	Received data	To 3101
4	Request to send	From 3101
5	Clear to send	To 3101
6	Data set ready	To 3101
7	Signal ground	N/A
8	Data carrier detect	To 3101
11	Supervisory transmitted data	From 3101
12	Supervisory received data	To 3101
20	Data terminal ready	From 3101

Company: IBM
Product: IBM PC
Port: Asynchronous Communications Adapter
Pin Configuration: C01

Pin	Function	Direction
2	Transmitted data	From PC
3	Received data	To PC
4	Request to send	From PC
5	Clear to send	To PC
6	Data set ready	To PC
7	Signal ground	N/A
8	Carrier detect	To PC
20	Data terminal ready	From PC
22	Ring indicator	To PC

Company: Infoscribe, Inc.
Product: 500 Printer
Port: Serial Interface   Pin Configuration: P04

Pin	Function	Direction
2	Received data	To 500
3	Received data	To 500
4	Request to send	From 500
7	Signal ground	N/A
10	Chassis ground	N/A
11	Busy	From 500

Notes: (a) Either pin 2 or pin 3 is used for incoming data, but not both. (b) Pin 11 is used for flow control.

Company: Integral Data Systems, Inc.
Product: Prism, 560, 460, 440, and 445 Printers
Port: Serial   Pin Configuration: P08

Pin	Function	Direction
1	Protective ground	N/A
2	Transmitted data	From printer
3	Received data	To printer
7	Signal ground	N/A
20	Data terminal ready	From printer
25	Fault (EIA level)	From printer

Notes: (a) 440 and 445 do not use XON/XOFF; the other printers do support it. (b) Pin 20 on all printers may be used for hardware flow control of the buffer status. (c) The fault signal (pin 25) is forced low when a paper-out or error condition is detected; otherwise it is high.

Company: Integrex, Inc.
Product: CX80 Printer
Port: RS-232   Pin Configuration: P07

Pin	Function	Direction
1	Protective ground	N/A
2	Transmitted data	From CX80
3	Received data	To CX80
6	Data set ready	To CX80
7	Signal ground	N/A
8	Data carrier detect	To CX80
11	Reverse channel	From CX80
20	Data terminal ready	From CX80

Notes: (a) Pins 6 and 8 must be high for the CX80 to receive data. (b) Pin 11 may be used for flow control. (c) The buffered version of this printer supports XON/XOFF and allows for pins 4 and 5 to be functional but removes pin 8 from the interface.

Company: Intelligent Systems Corp.
Product: 8000 Series
Port: J1   Pin Configuration: C08

Pin	Function	Direction
1	Protective ground	N/A
2	Transmitted data	From 8000
3	Received data	To 8000
4	Request to send	From 8000
7	Signal ground	N/A
20	Data terminal ready	From 8000

Notes: (a) Pins 4 and 20 are always high. (b) Port J2 is not RS-232-compatible. (c) A third RS-232-C I/O port may be installed offering pins 1–8 and 20, and clocking on pins 15, 17, and 24.

Company: Intelligent Systems Corp.
Product: Intecolor 3600 Computer
Port: Serial   Pin Configuration: C11

Pin	Function	Direction
1	Protective ground	N/A
2	Transmitted data	From 3600
3	Received data	To 3600
4	Request to send	From 3600
5	Clear to send	To 3600
7	Signal ground	N/A
20	Data terminal ready	From 3600

Company: Intertec Data Systems Corporation
Product: CompuStar and SuperBrain I/II
Port: Auxiliary   Pin Configuration: C12

Pin	Function	Direction
1	Protective ground	N/A
2	Received data	To computer
3	Transmitted data	From computer
7	Signal ground	N/A
20	Data terminal ready	To computer

Note: Pin 20 is used for flow control.

Company: Intertec Data Systems Corporation
Product: CompuStar and SuperBrain I/II
Port: Main   Pin Configuration: C01

Pin	Function	Direction
1	Protective ground	N/A
2	Transmitted data	From computer
3	Received data	To computer
4	Request to send	From computer
5	Clear to send	To computer
6	Data set ready	To computer
7	Signal ground	N/A
8	Data carrier detect	To computer
15	Transmit clock	To computer
17	Receive clock	To computer
20	Data terminal ready	From computer
22	Ring indicator	To computer
24	Clock (DTE source)	From computer

Company: Ithaca Intersystems, Inc.
Product: 6SIO Board
Port: RS-232   Pin Configuration: C09

Pin	Function	Direction
1	Ground	N/A
2	Transmitted data	To 6SIO
3	Received data	From 6SIO
4	Request to send	To 6SIO
5	Clear to send	From 6SIO
7	Signal ground	N/A
8	Rec. line signal detector	From 6SIO
20	Data terminal ready	To 6SIO

Note: Ports E and F provide timing on pin 15 in addition to the pins listed.

Company: Ithaca Intersystems, Inc.
Product: VIO Board
Port: RS-232   Pin Configuration: C09

Pin	Function	Direction
2	Transmitted data	To VIO
3	Received data	From VIO
4	Request to send	To VIO
5	Clear to send	From VIO
7	Signal ground	N/A
8	Rec. line signal detector	From VIO
20	Data set ready	To VIO

Notes: (a) This board may be used in the Ithaca 525 and 800 series computers. (b) Each port is configured as DCE for direct connection to a terminal.

Company: C. Itoh Electronics Inc.
Product: Comet I/II, Starwriter I/II, Prowriter I/II, and F10 Series Printers
Port: Serial   Pin Configuration: P06

Pin	Function	Direction
1	Frame ground	N/A
3	Received data	To printers
7	Signal ground	N/A
20	Data terminal ready	From printers

Note: Pin 20 can be used for the hardware XON/XOFF function. Software XON/XOFF is available on Prowriters and F10s only. In the latter case, pins 2, 4, 5, 6, and 8 are used normally.

Company: Juki Industries of America, Inc.
Product: 6100 Printer
Port: RS-232   Pin Configuration: P03

Pin	Function	Direction
1	Protective ground	N/A
2	Transmitted data	From 6100
3	Received data	To 6100
4	Request to send	From 6100
5	Clear to send	To 6100
6	Data set ready	To 6100
7	Signal ground	N/A
11	Secondary transmitted data	From 6100
20	Data terminal ready	From 6100

Notes: (a) XON/XOFF and ETX/ACK are supported. (b) Pin 20 may be used for hardware flow control.

Company: Lear Siegler, Inc.
Product: 310 Ballistic Printer
Port: Serial   Pin Configuration: P01

Pin	Function	Direction
1	Chassis ground	N/A
2	Transmitted data	From 310
3	Received data	To 310
4	Request to send	From 310
5	Clear to send	To 310
6	Data set ready	To 310
7	Signal ground	N/A
8	Carrier detect	To 310
14	Busy	From 310
15	External transmit clock	To 310
17	External receive clock	To 310
19	Busy	From 310
20	Data terminal ready	From 310

Note: This connection is via a cable from the J5 interface.

Company: Lear Siegler, Inc.
Product: ADM-5 and ADM-3A
Port: Modem   Pin Configuration: T04

Pin	Function	Direction
1	Protective ground	N/A
2	Transmitted data	From ADM
3	Received data	To ADM
4	Request to send	From ADM
5	Clear to send	To ADM
7	Signal ground	N/A
8	Carrier detect	To ADM
11	Secondary channel control	From ADM
12	Secondary received data	To ADM
20	Data terminal ready	From ADM

Company: Lear Siegler, Inc.
Product: ADM-31, ADM-32, and ADM-42
Port: Modem   Pin Configuration: T01

Pin	Function	Direction
1	Equipment ground	N/A
2	Transmitted data	From ADM
3	Received data	To ADM
4	Request to send	From ADM
5	Clear to send	To ADM
6	Data set ready	To ADM
7	Signal ground	N/A
8	Data carrier detect	To ADM
19	Secondary request to send	From ADM
20	Data terminal ready	From ADM

Company: Malibu Electronics Corp.
Product: Dual-Mode 200 Printer
Port: Serial   Pin Configuration: P03

Pin	Function	Direction
1	Chassis ground	N/A
2	Transmitted data	From 200
3	Received data	To 200
4	Request to send	From 200
5	Clear to send	To 200
7	Signal ground	N/A
20	Data terminal ready	From 200

Note: Pin 20 may be used for flow control, even though XON/XOFF is supported.

Company: Mannesmann Tally Corp.
Product: MT-180 and MT-160 Printers
Port: RS-232-C   Pin Configuration: P07

Pin	Function	Direction
1	Chassis ground	N/A
2	Transmitted data	From printer
3	Received data	To printer
7	Signal ground	N/A
11	Busy	From printer
19	Busy	From printer
20	Data terminal ready	From printer

Notes: (a) Pins 11 and 19 may be used for hardware flow control. (b) The printers support both the XON/XOFF and ETX/ACK protocols.

Company: Mannesmann Tally Corp.
Product: MT-1605, MT-1705, and MT-1805 Printers
Port: RS-232   Pin Configuration: P07

Pin	Function	Direction
1	Chassis ground	N/A
2	Transmitted data	From printer
3	Received data	To printer
5	Clear to send	To printer
6	Data set ready	To printer
7	Signal ground	N/A
11	Busy	From printer
19	Busy	From printer
20	Data terminal ready	From printer

Notes: (a) Pins 11 and 19 may be used for hardware flow control. (b) The printers support XON/XOFF characters.

Company: Mannesmann Tally Corp.
Product: MT-1612 Printer Terminal
Port: RS-232-C   Pin Configuration: P01

Pin	Function	Direction
1	Protective ground	N/A
2	Transmitted data	From 1612
3	Received data	To 1612
4	Request to send	From 1612
5	Clear to send	To 1612
5	Data set ready	To 1612
7	Signal ground	N/A
8	Rec. line signal detector	To 1612
11	Secondary request to send	From 1612
12	Secondary RLSD	To 1612
19	Secondary request to send	From 1612
20	Data terminal ready	From 1612
22	Ring indicator	To 1612

Notes: (a) Pins 11 and 19 may be used for flow control. (b) Terminal supports XON/XOFF protocol.

Company: Mannesmann Tally Corp.
Product: Tally 2000 Printer
Port: TTY Serial   Pin Configuration: P05

Pin	Function	Direction
1	Chassis ground	N/A
3	Received data	To 2000
4	Request to send	From 2000
6	Data set ready	To 2000
7	Signal ground	N/A
8	Data carrier detect	To 2000
11	Supervisory transmitted data	From 2000
20	Data terminal ready	From 2000
22	Ring indicator	To 2000

Notes: (a) Pin 4 is held off, maintaining the printer in the receive mode. (b) Pin 11 should be used for flow control.

Company: Mannesmann Tally Corp.
Product: T-3000 Printer
Port: ACA Interface   Pin Configuration: P05

Pin	Function	Direction
1	Chassis ground	N/A
2	Transmitted data	From T-3000
3	Received data	To T-3000
4	Request to send	From T-3000
5	Clear to send	To T-3000
6	Data set ready	To T-3000
7	Signal ground	N/A
11	Reverse channel	From T-3000
20	Data terminal ready	From T-3000

Notes: (a) Pin 11 should be used for hardware flow control. (b) This printer also supports the XON/XOFF and ENQ/ACK protocols.

Company: Megatek Corporation
Product: Whizzard 7200 Terminal
Port: Serial   Pin Configuration: T04

Pin	Function	Direction
1	Protective ground	N/A
2	Transmitted data	From 7200
3	Received data	To 7200
4	Request to send	From 7200
5	Clear to send	To 7200
7	Signal ground	N/A
8	Data carrier detect	To 7200
20	Data terminal ready	From 7200

Note: Pin 5 must be received to enable the transmission of data.

Company: Microdata Corporation
Product: Reality
Port: Terminal   Pin Configuration: C02

Pin	Function	Direction
1	Protective ground	N/A
2	Transmitted data	To Reality
3	Received data	From Reality
5	Clear to send	From Reality
7	Signal ground	N/A
8	Data carrier detect	From Reality
20	Data terminal ready	To Reality

Note: Pins 5, 8 and 20 are all jumpered together.

Company: Micro Technology Unlimited
Product: MTU-130 Computer
Port: Serial   Pin Configuration: C01

Pin	Function	Direction
1	Frame ground	N/A
2	Transmitted data	From MTU-130
3	Received data	To MTU-130
4	Request to send	From MTU-130
5	Clear to send	To MTU-130
6	Data set ready	To MTU-130
7	Signal ground	N/A
8	Carrier detect	To MTU-130
20	Data terminal ready	From MTU-130

Company: Microtek, Inc.
Product: MT-80S Printer
Port: Serial   Pin Configuration: P08

Pin	Function	Direction
1	Chassis ground	N/A
2	Received data	To printer
5	Clear to send	From printer
7	DC common	N/A
20	Data terminal ready	From printer

Note: Pin 5 or pin 20 may be used for flow control.

Company: Mitsubishi Electronics America, Inc.
Product: Multi-16 Personal Computer
Port: RS-232   Pin Configuration: C01

Pin	Function	Direction
1	Frame ground	N/A
2	Transmitted data	From Multi-16
3	Received data	To Multi-16
4	Request to send	From Multi-16
5	Clear to send	To Multi-16
6	Data set ready	To Multi-16
7	Signal ground	N/A
8	Data carrier detect	To Multi-16
15	Transmit timing	To Multi-16
17	Receive timing	To Multi-16
20	Data terminal ready	From Multi-16
24	Timing (DTE source)	From Multi-16

Note: Various signal directions can be changed by means of option switches.

Company: Mountain Computer Inc.
Product: CPS Multifunction Card
Port: Serial   Pin Configuration: C01

Pin	Function	Direction
1	Protective ground	N/A
2	Transmitted data	From CPS
3	Received data	To CPS
4	Request to send	From CPS
5	Clear to send	To CPS
6	Data set ready	To CPS
7	Signal ground	N/A
8	Data carrier detect	To CPS
20	Data terminal ready	From CPS

Notes: (a) Pin 5 must be high before incoming data will be accepted. (b) Pin 8 must be high before transmitting or receiving data. (c) Pin 6 must be high before transmitting or receiving data.

Company: NEC Information Systems, Inc.
Product: 3500R Printer
Port: Serial   Pin Configuration: P13

Pin	Function	Direction
2	Transmitted data	From printer
3	Received data	To printer
4	Request to send	From printer
6	Data set ready	To printer
7	Signal ground	N/A
19	Reverse channel	From printer
20	Data terminal ready	From printer

Notes: (a) Pin 6 must be on for the printer to operate. (b) Pin 19 can be used for flow control, but polarity must be checked.

Company: NEC Information Systems, Inc.
Product: 3500 Series (except 3500R) and 7700 Series Printers
Port: Serial   Pin Configuration: P01

Pin	Function	Direction
2	Transmitted data	From printer
3	Received data	To printer
4	Request to send	From printer
5	Clear to send	To printer
6	Data set ready	To printer
7	Signal ground	N/A
8	Carrier detect	To printer
11	Reset	To printer
18	Keyboard inhibit	To printer
19	Reverse channel	From printer
20	Data terminal ready	From printer
21	Print inhibit	To printer
22	Buzzer	To printer
23	Paper out/ribbon end	From printer
25	Interrupt/break	From printer

Notes: (a) Pins 5, 6, and 8 must be on before the printers will operate. (b) Pin 19 can be used for flow control, but the correct polarity must be chosen.

Company: NEC Information Systems, Inc.
Product: Advanced Personal Computer
Port: Serial   Pin Configuration: C01

Pin	Function	Direction
1	Signal ground	N/A
2	Transmitted data	From APC
3	Received data	To APC
4	Request to send	From APC
5	Clear to send	To APC
6	Data set ready	To APC
7	Signal ground	N/A
15	Transmit clock	To APC
17	Receive clock	To APC
20	Data terminal ready	From APC
24	Transmit clock	From APC

Company: NEC Information Systems, Inc.
Product: PC8001A Computer
Port: Serial   Pin Configuration: C01

Pin	Function	Direction
1	Signal ground	N/A
2	Transmitted data	From PC
3	Received data	To PC
4	Request to send	From PC
5	Clear to send	To PC
6	Data set ready	To PC
7	Carrier detect	To PC
8	Data terminal ready	From PC
9	Signal ground	N/A

Note: This connector is on the rear of the PC8001. It is recommended that a cable be built to convert this circular connector to the standard-size connector with the corresponding pin assignments.

Company: North Star Computers, Inc.
Product: Advantage Computer
Port: Serial   Pin Configuration: C01

Pin	Function	Direction
1	Chassis ground	N/A
2	Transmitted data	From Advantage
3	Received data	To Advantage
4	Request to send	From Advantage
5	Clear to send	To Advantage
6	Data set ready	To Advantage
7	Signal ground	N/A
8	Carrier detect	To Advantage
17	Receive clock	To Advantage
20	Data terminal ready	From Advantage
24	Transmit clock	From Advantage

Company: North Star Computers, Inc.
Product: Horizon Computer System
Port: Serial   Pin Configuration: C01

Pin	Function	Direction
1	Chassis ground	N/A
2	Transmitted data	From Horizon
3	Received data	To Horizon
4	Request to send	From Horizon
5	Clear to send	To Horizon
6	Data set ready	To Horizon
7	Signal ground	N/A
8	Carrier detect	To Horizon
15	Transmit clock	To Horizon
17	Receive clock	To Horizon
20	Data terminal ready	From Horizon
24	Transmit clock	From Horizon

Company: Okidata Corporation
Product: Microline 82/83 and 82A/83A Printers
Port: High-speed RS-232-C   Pin Configuration: P05

Pin	Function	Direction
1	Protective ground	N/A
2	Transmitted data	From printer
3	Received data	To printer
4	Request to send	From printer
5	Clear to send	To printer
6	Data set ready	To printer
7	Signal ground	N/A
8	Carrier detect	To printer
11	Supervisory transmitted data	From printer
20	Data terminal ready	From printer

Notes: (a) Pin 11 can be used for flow control and to check polarity. (b) Pin 20 can be used for paper-out indicator. (c) Pins 5, 6, and 8 should be on to allow data reception.

Company: Olivetti OPE
Product: TH 240 Printer
Port: Serial   Pin Configuration: P03

Pin	Function	Direction
1	Protective ground	N/A
2	Transmitted data	From printer
3	Received data	To printer
4	Request to send	From printer
6	Data set ready	To printer
7	Signal ground	N/A
8	Rec. line signal detector	To printer
11	Reverse channel	From printer
14	Secondary transmitted data	From printer
19	Secondary request to send	From printer
20	Data terminal ready	From printer

Notes: (a) Pin 2, 11, or 14 may be used for flow control. (b) Pin 20 goes off when anomaly conditions occur.

Company: Olympia USA Inc.
Product: ES101 KRO Printer
Port: Serial   Pin Configuration: P03

Pin	Function	Direction
1	Protective ground	N/A
2	Transmitted data	From 101
3	Received data	To 101
4	Request to send	From 101
20	Data terminal ready	From 101

Notes: (a) Request to send can be optioned to occur on pin 4, 5, 6, 8, or 20. (b) Pin 20 can be used for flow control, in which case it cannot be used for request to send because a conflict will occur.

Company: Olympia USA Inc.
Product: ESW 102/103 Printers
Port: RS-232-C   Pin Configuration: P12

Pin	Function	Direction
2	Transmitted data	From printer
3	Received data	To printer
4	Request to send	From printer
5	Clear to send	To printer
7	Signal ground	N/A

Notes: (a) Pin 4 is used for flow control when XON/XOFF is not selected. (b) Note that there is no pin 20.

Company: Osborne Computer Corp.
Product: Osborne 1
Port: Serial RS-232   Pin Configuration: C09

Pin	Function	Direction
1	Ground	N/A
2	Transmitted data	To Osborne
3	Received data	From Osborne
4	Request to send	To Osborne
5	Clear to send	From Osborne
6	Data set ready	From Osborne
7	Signal ground	N/A
8	Carrier detect	From Osborne
20	Data terminal ready	To Osborne

Note: Pins 5, 6, and 8 are held at +5 volts.

Company: OSM Computer Corp.
Product: Zeus Computer
Port: RS-232-C   Pin Configuration: C07

Pin	Function	Direction
2	Transmitted data	From Zeus
3	Received data	To Zeus
7	Signal ground	N/A
20	Data terminal ready	From Zeus

Note: Each SIO board has A and B ports that have the same pins.

Company: Otrona Corporation
Product: ATTACHE Computer
Port: Serial   Pin Configuration: C09

Pin	Function	Direction
1	Protective ground	N/A
2	Transmitted data	To ATTACHE
3	Received data	From ATTACHE
5	Clear to send	From ATTACHE
6	Data set ready	From ATTACHE
7	Signal ground	N/A
8	Rec. line signal detector	From ATTACHE
20	Data terminal ready	To ATTACHE

Note: The interface is provided by an Otrona-provided cable. A different cable allows the Attache to be directly connected to a modem.

Company: Panasonic
Product: HHC Computer
Port: Serial   Pin Configuration: C01

Pin	Function	Direction
1	Frame ground	N/A
2	Transmitted data (red)	From HHC
3	Received data (orange)	To HHC
4	Request to send (yellow)	From HHC
5	Clear to send (green)	To HHC
6	Data set ready (blue)	To HHC
7	Signal ground	N/A
8	Rec. line sig. det. (gray)	To HHC
20	Data terminal ready	From HHC

Note: Wire color is indicated beside each function.

Company: Perkin-Elmer Corporation
Product: 550 and 1251 CRTs
Port: Serial   Pin Configuration: T01

Pin	Function	Direction
1	Protective ground	N/A
2	Transmitted data	From CRT
3	Received data	To CRT
4	Request to send	From CRT
5	Clear to send	To CRT
6	Data set ready	To CRT
7	Signal ground	N/A
8	Carrier detect	To CRT
20	Data terminal ready	From CRT

Company: Personal Micro Computers, Inc.
Product: PMC-80/81
Port: RS-232-C   Pin Configuration: C01

Pin	Function	Direction
1	Protective ground	N/A
2	Transmitted data	From PMC
3	Received data	To PMC
4	Request to send	From PMC
5	Clear to send	To PMC
6	Data set ready	To PMC
7	Signal ground	N/A
8	Carrier detect	To PMC
20	Data terminal ready	From PMC
22	Ring indicator	To PMC

Company: Pertec Computer Corporation
Product: PCC 2000 Computers
Port: RS-232   Pin Configuration: C15

Pin	Function	Direction
2	Received data	To 2000
3	Transmitted data	From 2000
4	Request to send	From 2000
5	Clear to send	To 2000
7	Signal ground	N/A
8	Data carrier detect	To 2000
20	Data terminal ready	From 2000

Notes: (a) Pin 4 is a handshake signal for controlling data from the attached external device. (b) Pin 5 is a signal for controlling the transmitting of data to the external device.

Company: Pertec Computer Corporation
Product: Pertec 3000
Port: COM0/COM1/COM2   Pin Configuration: C01

Pin	Function	Direction
2	Transmitted data	From 3000
3	Received data	To 3000
4	Request to send	From 3000
5	Clear to send	To 3000
6	Data set ready	To 3000
7	Signal ground	N/A
8	Data carrier detect	To 3000
15	Transmit clock	To 3000
17	Receive clock	To 3000
20	Data terminal ready	From 3000

Company: Printek, Inc.
Product: 910/920 Printers
Port: RS-232   Pin Configuration: P05

Pin	Function	Direction
1	Chassis ground	N/A
2	Transmitted data	From printer
3	Received data	To printer
4	Request to send	From printer
5	Clear to send	To printer
6	Data set ready	To printer
7	Signal ground	N/A
8	Carrier detect	To printer
11	Busy	From printer
20	Data terminal ready	From printer

Notes: (a) XON/XOFF and ETX/ACK are supported. (b) Pin 11 is used for hardware flow control.

Company: Printronix
Product: Printronix 300 Printer
Port: RS-232   Pin Configuration: P05

Pin	Function	Direction
1	Protective ground	N/A
3	Received data (in)	To 300
4	Request to send (out)	From 300
6	Data set ready (in)	To 300
7	Signal ground	N/A
8	Carrier detect (in)	To 300
11	Reverse channel (out)	From 300
20	Data terminal ready (out)	From 300
25	External clock (in)	To 300

Company: Prometheus Products, Inc.
Product: VERSAcard
Port: Serial   Pin Configuration: C01

Pin	Function	Direction
1	Protective ground	N/A
2	Transmitted data	From Versacard
3	Received data	To Versacard
4	Request to send	From Versacard
5	Clear to send	To Versacard
6	Data set ready	To Versacard
7	Signal ground	N/A
20	Data terminal ready	From Versacard

Notes; (a) Pin 5 should be used for flow control. (b) Pin 6 must be on before VERSAcard will receive data.

Company: Quantex Division of North Atlantic Industries
Product: Series 6000 Printer
Port: Serial   Pin Configuration: P07

Pin	Function	Direction
1	Chassis ground	N/A
2	Transmitted data (out)	From 6000
3	Received data (in)	To 6000
7	Signal ground	N/A
11	Busy	From 6000
14	Busy	From 6000
20	Ready	From 6000

Notes: (a) XON/XOFF is supported. (b) Pin 11 or pin 14 may be used for hardware flow control. (c) Pin 20 indicates the status of "hold."

Company: Qume Corporation
Product: Sprint 5
Port: Serial   Pin Configuration: P03

Pin	Function	Direction
1	Chassis/frame ground	N/A
2	Transmitted data	From Sprint 5
3	Received data	To Sprint 5
4	Request to send	From Sprint 5
5	Clear to send	To Sprint 5
6	Data set ready	To Sprint 5
7	Signal ground	N/A
8	Carrier detect	To Sprint 5
20	Data terminal ready	From Sprint 5

Notes: (a) Pins 20 and 4 both serve the same function of hardware flow control. (b) Pin 5 must be high for data transmission. (c) Pin 6 must be high for data reception.

Company: Qume Corporation
Product: Sprint 9/45 and 9/55
Port: RS-232-C   Pin Configuration: P03

Pin	Function	Direction
1	Chassis ground	N/A
2	Transmitted data	From Sprint
3	Received data	To Sprint
4	Request to send	From Sprint
5	Clear to send	To Sprint
6	Data set ready	To Sprint
7	Signal ground	N/A
8	Carrier detect	To Sprint
20	Data terminal ready	From Sprint

Notes: (a) Pin 20 can be used for hardwired handshaking. (b) XON/XOFF handshaking is supported for flow control.

Company: Radio Shack
Product: DT-1 CRT
Port: EIA   Pin Configuration: T01

Pin	Function	Direction
1	Protective ground	N/A
2	Transmitted data	From DT-1
3	Received data	To DT-1
4	Request to send	From DT-1
5	Clear to send	To DT-1
6	Data set ready	To DT-1
7	Signal ground	N/A
8	Data carrier detect	To DT-1
20	Data terminal ready	From DT-1

Company: Radio Shack
Product: Line Printer VII/VIII
Port: RS-232-C   Pin Configuration: P14

Pin	Function	Direction
2	Transmitted data	To printer
7	Signal ground	N/A
8	Data carrier detect	From printer

Note: The printers come with a DIN connector that should first be wired to an RS-232-size plug. Pin 8 may then be used for flow control.

Company: Radio Shack
Product: TRS-80 Model I
Port: EIA   Pin Configuration: C01

Pin	Function	Direction
1	Protective ground	N/A
2	Transmitted data	From TRS-80
3	Received data	To TRS-80
4	Request to send	From TRS-80
5	Clear to send	To TRS-80
6	Data set ready	To TRS-80
7	Signal ground	N/A
8	Data carrier detect	To TRS-80
20	Data terminal ready	From TRS-80

Company: Radio Shack
Product: TRS-80 Model II
Port: Channels A and B   Pin Configuration: C01

Pin	Function	Direction
1	Protective ground	N/A
2	Transmitted data	From TRS-80
3	Received data	To TRS-80
4	Request to send	From TRS-80
5	Clear to send	To TRS-80
6	Data set ready	To TRS-80
7	Signal ground	N/A
8	Carrier detect	To TRS-80
15	I/O transmit S.E.T.	To TRS-80
17	Receive clock	To TRS-80
20	Data terminal ready	From TRS-80
24	Transmit clock	From TRS-80

Note: Channel A allows asynchronous or synchronous transmission. Channel B has the same signals but lacks pins 15 and 24 and consequently supports only asynchronous transmission.

Company: Radio Shack
Product: TRS-80 Model III
Port: P1   Pin Configuration: C01

Pin	Function	Direction
1	Protective ground	N/A
2	Transmitted data	From TRS-80
3	Received data	To TRS-80
4	Request to send	From TRS-80
5	Clear to send	To TRS-80
6	Data set ready	To TRS-80
7	Signal ground	N/A
8	Carrier detect	To TRS-80
20	Data terminal ready	From TRS-80
22	Ring indicator	To TRS-80

Company: Radio Shack
Product: Model 16 Computer
Port: Channels A and B   Pin Configuration: C11

Pin	Function	Direction
1	Protective ground	N/A
2	Transmitted data	From Model 16
3	Received data	To Model 16
4	Request to send	From Model 16
5	Clear to send	To Model 16
7	Signal ground	N/A
8	Carrier detect	To Model 16
15	I/O transmit timing	To Model 16
17	Receive timing	To Model 16
20	Data terminal ready	From Model 16
24	Transmit clock	From Model 16

Note: Channel A allows asynchronous or synchronous transmission. Channel B has the same signals but lacks pins 15 and 24 and consequently supports only asynchronous transmission.

Company: Rogers Products Company, Inc.
Product: Typrinter
Port: Serial   Pin Configuration: P10

Pin	Function	Direction
1	Protective ground	N/A
2	Transmitted data	From printer
3	Received data	To printer
4	Request to send	From printer
5	Clear to send	To printer
6	Data set ready	To printer
7	Signal ground	N/A
8	Carrier detect	To printer
20	Data terminal ready	From printer

Notes: (a) This is the DTE connector. A DCE connector is available that reverses most of the leads. (b) XON/XOFF is supported.

Company: R2E of America
Product: Micral 9050 Computer
Port: V.24 (RS-232)   Pin Configuration: C11

Pin	Function	Direction
1	Ground	N/A
2	Transmitted data	From 9050
3	Receive data	To 9050
4	Request to send	From 9050
5	Clear to send	To 9050
7	Logic ground	N/A
8	Carrier detect	To 9050
15	Transmit clock	To 9050
17	Receive clock	To 9050
20	Data terminal ready	From 9050
24	Transmit clock	From 9050

Note: All serial channels are wired identically.

Company: Santec Corp.
Product: Variflex Printer
Port: RS-232   Pin Configuration: P05

Pin	Function	Direction
1	Protective ground	N/A
2	Transmitted data	From Variflex
3	Received data	To Variflex
4	Request to send	From Variflex
5	Clear to send	To Variflex
6	Data set ready	To Variflex
7	Signal ground	N/A
8	Carrier detect	To Variflex
11	Busy	From Variflex
20	Data terminal ready	From Variflex

Notes: (a) The Variflex supports XON/XOFF or ETX/ACK pacing. (b) Either pin 11 or pin 20 may be used for hardware flow control.

Company: Siemens Corporation
Product: 2712 and PT 80 I2 Printers
Port: EIA   Pin Configuration: P15

Pin	Function	Direction
1	Common return	N/A
2	Transmitted data	From printer
3	Received data	To printer
4	Request to send	From printer
5	Clear to send	To printer
6	Data set ready	To printer
7	Signal ground	N/A
8	Rec. line signal detector	To printer
20	Data terminal ready	From printer
25	Busy	From printer

Notes: (a) Pin 25 could be used for flow control. (b) These devices do support XON/XOFF.

Company: Siemens Corporation
Product: OEM Ink-jet Printer Models 2712 and PT 80 I2
Port: RS-232   Pin Configuration: P15

Pin	Function	Direction
1	Common return	N/A
2	Transmitted data	From printer
3	Received data	To printer
4	Request to send	From printer
5	Clear to send	To printer
6	Data set ready	To printer
7	Signal ground	N/A
8	Data channel RLSD	To printer
20	Data terminal ready	From printer
25	Busy	From printer

Notes: (a) Pin 25 can be used for hardware flow control. (b) XON/XOFF capability exists.

Company: Smith-Corona
Product: TP-1 Printer
Port: Serial   Pin Configuration: P09

Pin	Function	Direction
3	Received data	To TP-1
4	Request to send	From TP-1
7	Signal ground	N/A
20	Data terminal ready	From TP-1

Note: Pin 4 or 20 may be used as the busy signal for flow control.

Company: Silver-Reed
Product: Silver-Reed
Port: RS-232   Pin Configuration: P03

Pin	Function	Direction
1	Protective ground	N/A
2	Transmitted data	From printer
3	Received data	To printer
4	Request to send	From printer
5	Clear to send	To printer
7	Signal ground	N/A
20	Data terminal ready	From printer

Notes: (a) Pin 20 is used for hardware flow control. (b) This interface is the DTF01S, manufactured by Wilker, Inc.

Company: Southwest Technical Products Corp.
Product: MP-S2 Dual Serial Interface
Port: A and B   Pin Configuration: C14

Pin	Function	Direction
1	Ground	N/A
2	Received data	To MP-S2
3	Transmitted data	From MP-S2
4	Request to send	To MP-S2
5	Clear to send	From MP-S2
7	Ground	N/A
8	Data carrier detect	From MP-S2
12	Secondary DCD	To MP-S2
19	Hold down	To MP-S2
20	Clear to send	To MP-S2
24	Clock in	To MP-S2

Notes: (a) Pins 4 and 5 are tied together internally so that when the attached device turns on RTS, CTS is immediately given back. (b) Pin 19 is used with the SWTPC CT-82 terminal to indicate that a key is being held down on the keyboard. (c) Pin 20 should be used for flow control.

Company: SSM Microcomputer Products, Inc.
Product: AIO-II
Port: Serial (J3)   Pin Configuration: C14

Pin	Function	Direction
1	Frame ground	N/A
2	Transmitted data	To AIO
3	Received data	From AIO
4	Request to send	To AIO
5	Clear to send	From AIO
6	Data set ready	From AIO
7	Signal ground	N/A
8	Data carrier detect	From AIO
20	Data terminal ready	To AIO

Note: Either pin 4 or pin 20 may be used for hardware flow control.

Company: SSM Microcomputer Products, Inc.
Product: AIO-II
Port: Serial (J4)   Pin Configuration: C01

Pin	Function	Direction
1	Frame ground	N/A
2	Transmitted data	From AIO
3	Received data	To AIO
4	Request to send	From AIO
5	Clear to send	To AIO
6	Data set ready	To AIO
7	Signal ground	N/A
8	Data carrier detect	To AIO
20	Data terminal ready	From AIO

Company: SSM Microcomputer Products, Inc.
Product: ASIO
Port: J1 (DTE)   Pin Configuration: C14

Pin	Function	Direction
1	Frame ground	N/A
2	Transmitted data	To ASIO
3	Received data	From ASIO
4	Request to send	To ASIO
5	Clear to send	From ASIO
6	Data set ready	From ASIO
7	Signal ground	N/A
8	Data carrier detect	From ASIO
20	Data terminal ready	To ASIO

Notes: (a) A cable connects to J1 to provide the DB25 connector. (b) Pins 6 and 8 are pulled up to +12 volts. (c) Pin 4 or pin 20 may be used for the busy signal from the attached device.

Company: SSM Microcomputer Products, Inc.
Product: ASIO
Port: J2 (DCE)   Pin Configuration: C01

Pin	Function	Direction
1	Frame ground	N/A
2	Transmitted data	From ASIO
3	Received data	To ASIO
4	Request to send	From ASIO
5	Clear to send	To ASIO
7	Signal ground	N/A
8	Data carrier detect	To ASIO
20	Data terminal ready	From ASIO

Notes: (a) A cable connects to J2 to provide the DB25 connector. (b) Pin 5 should be used as a busy detector signal and should be connected to the flow control signal of the hardware of the attached device.

Company: SSM Microcomputer Products, Inc.
Product: AIO
Port: Serial   Pin Configuration: C01

Pin	Function	Direction
1	Frame ground	N/A
2	Transmitted data	From AIO
3	Received data	To AIO
4	Request to send	From AIO
5	Clear to send	To AIO
7	Signal ground	N/A
8	Data carrier detect	To AIO
20	Data terminal ready	From AIO

Note: Pin 5 should be connected to the device's busy signal lead, as it must be on for the AIO to transmit data.

Company: Star Micronics, Inc.
Product: DP-8480 Printer
Port: RS-232   Pin Configuration: P04

Pin	Function	Direction
1	Protective ground	N/A
3	Received data	To DP-8480
4	Request to send	From DP-8480
7	Signal ground	N/A
11	Busy status output	From DP-8480
20	Data terminal ready	From DP-8480

Notes: (a) This interface is for printers with serial numbers 20004833 and higher. (b) These printers use pin 11 for hardware flow control.

Company: Tarbell Electronics
Product: Empire Computer
Port: A/B on I/O Board   Pin Configuration: C01

Pin	Function	Direction
2	Transmitted data	From Empire
3	Received data	To Empire
4	Request to send	From Empire
5	Clear to send	To Empire
6	Data set ready	To Empire
7	Signal ground	N/A
20	Data terminal ready	From Empire

Notes: (a) Pin 6 is monitored for handshaking from printers. It should be connected to the flow control lead of the printer being connected. (b) Port A is normally used for a CRT, while port B is used to attach a printer.

Company: Tektronix, Inc.
Product: 4050 CRT Series
Port: RS-232-C   Pin Configuration: T01

Pin	Function	Direction
1	Protective ground	N/A
2	Transmitted data	From 4050
3	Received data	To 4050
4	Request to send	From 4050
5	Clear to send	To 4050
6	Data set ready	To 4050
7	Signal ground	N/A
8	Data carrier detect	To 4050
11	Secondary request to send	From 4050
12	Secondary RLSD	To 4050
19	Secondary request to send	From 4050
20	Data terminal ready	From 4050

Note: Models 4052 and 4054 allow for external clocking on pins 24 and 25.

Company: Tektronix, Inc.
Product: 4643 Printer
Port: Serial   Pin Configuration: P03

Pin	Function	Direction
1	Protective ground	N/A
2	Transmitted data	From 4643
3	Received data	To 4643
4	Request to send	From 4643
7	Signal ground	N/A
8	Rec. line signal detector	To 4643
20	Data terminal ready	From 4643

Note: Pin 20 may be used for hardware flow control.

Company: Teletype Corp.
Product: DataSpeed 40/2 Terminal
Port: Comm.   Pin Configuration: T01

Pin	Function	Direction
1	Protective ground	N/A
2	Transmitted data	From 40/2
3	Received data	To 40/2
4	Request to send	From 40/2
5	Clear to send	To 40/2
6	Data set ready	To 40/2
7	Signal ground	N/A
8	Rec. line signal detector	To 40/2
11	Secondary request to send	From 40/2
12	Secondary RLSD	To 40/2
19	Secondary request to send	From 40/2
20	Data terminal ready	From 40/2
22	Ring indicator	To 40/2

Note: If this port is optioned for full-duplex, pins 4, 11, and 19 are not present.

Company: Teletype Corp.
Product: DataSpeed 40 Printer
Port: RS-232   Pin Configuration: P05

Pin	Function	Direction
1	Protective ground	N/A
2	Transmitted data	From 40
3	Received data	To 40
4	Request to send	From 40
5	Clear to send	To 40
6	Data set ready	To 40
7	Signal ground	N/A
8	Data carrier detect	To 40
11	Supervisory transmitted data	From 40
12	Supervisory received data	To 40
20	Data terminal ready	From 40
22	Ring indicator	To 40
23	Alarm	

Company: Teletype Corp.
Product: DataSpeed 4420 Terminal
Port: Modem   Pin Configuration: T01

Pin	Function	Direction
1	Frame ground	N/A
2	Transmitted data	From 4420
3	Received data	To 4420
4	Request to send	From 4420
5	Clear to send	To 4420
6	Data set ready	To 4420
7	Signal ground	N/A
8	Rec. line signal detector	To 4420
11	Secondary request to send	From 4420
12	Secondary RLSD	To 4420
15	Transmit timing	To 4420
17	Receive timing	To 4420
19	Secondary request to send	From 4420
20	Data terminal ready	From 4420
22	Ring indicator	To 4420

Company: Teletype Corp.
Product: DataSpeed AP200 Printer
Port: EIA   Pin Configuration: P11

Pin	Function	Direction
1	Frame ground	N/A
3	Received data	To AP200
6	Data set ready	To AP200
7	Signal ground	N/A
11	Secondary transmitted data	From AP200
14	Device next character	From AP200
19	Secondary request to send	From AP200
20	Data terminal ready	From AP200

Notes: (a) Pins 11 and 20 are equivalent in function: Both indicate that the printer is able to receive. (b) Pin 14 has a positive voltage when the buffer is less than 3/4 full and a negative voltage when buffer is more than 3/4 full.

Company: Teletype Corp.
Product: Model 43 Teleprinter
Port: EIA   Pin Configuration: P03

Pin	Function	Direction
1	Protective ground	N/A
2	Transmitted data	From 43
3	Received data	To 43
4	Request to send	From 43
5	Clear to send	To 43
6	Data set ready	To 43
7	Signal ground	N/A
8	Carrier detect/RLSD	To 43
20	Data terminal ready	From 43
22	Ring indicator	To 43

Note: Pin 20 is affected by the paper supply.

Company: Televideo Systems, Inc.
Product: Model 910, 925, and 950 CRTs
Port: P3 Connector   Pin Configuration: T01

Pin	Function	Direction
1	Frame ground	N/A
2	Transmitted data (out)	From CRT
3	Received data (in)	To CRT
4	Request to send	From CRT
5	Clear to send	To CRT
6	Data set ready	To CRT
7	Signal ground	N/A
8	Data carrier detect	To CRT
20	Data terminal ready	From CRT

Company: Televideo Systems, Inc.
Product: TS800A, TS802, and TS80H Computers
Port: P1 (DTE)   Pin Configuration: C01

Pin	Function	Direction
1	Frame ground	N/A
2	Transmitted data	From computer
3	Received data	To computer
4	Request to send	From computer
5	Clear to send	To computer
7	Signal ground	N/A
8	Data carrier detect	To computer
15	Transmit timing	To computer
17	Receive timing	To computer
20	Data terminal ready	From computer
24	Transmit timing	From computer

Company: Televideo Systems, Inc.
Product: TS800A, TS802, and TS802H Computers
Port: P2 (Serial Printer)   Pin Configuration: C14

Pin	Function	Direction
1	Frame ground	N/A
2	Received data	To computer
3	Transmitted data	From computer
4	Request to send	To computer
5	Clear to send	From computer
6	Data set ready	From computer
7	Signal ground	N/A
8	Data carrier detect	From computer
20	Busy	To computer

Note: Pin 20 should be used for flow control.

Company: Televideo Systems, Inc.
Product: TS806 Computer
Port: P2   Pin Configuration: C11

Pin	Function	Direction
1	Frame ground	N/A
2	Transmitted data	From TS806
3	Received data	To TS806
4	Request to send	From TS806
5	Clear to send	To TS806
7	Signal ground	N/A
8	Data carrier detect	To TS806
20	Data terminal ready	From TS806

Company: Televideo Systems, Inc.
Product: TS806 Computer
Port: P3 (DCE)   Pin Configuration: C14

Pin	Function	Direction
1	Frame ground	N/A
2	Received data	To TS806
3	Transmitted data	From TS806
4	Request to send	To TS806
5	Clear to send	From TS806
7	Signal ground	N/A
8	Data carrier detect	From TS806
20	Data terminal ready	To TS806

Note: Pin 20 should be used for a printer busy indicator.

Company: Televideo Systems, Inc.
Product: TS816
Port: P2 (Terminal), P8 (Serial Printer)   Pin Configuration: C14

Pin	Function	Direction
1	Frame ground	N/A
2	Received data	To TS816
3	Transmitted data	From TS816
4	Request to send	To TS816
5	Clear to send	From TS816
7	Signal ground	N/A
8	Data carrier detect	From TS816
20	Data terminal ready	To TS816

Note: Pin 20 is usually used for flow control.

Company: Televideo Systems, Inc.
Product: TS816 Computer
Port: P9 (Modem)   Pin Configuration: C01

Pin	Function	Direction
1	Frame ground	N/A
2	Transmitted data	From TS816
3	Received data	To TS816
4	Request to send	From TS816
5	Clear to send	To TS816
7	Signal ground	N/A
8	Data carrier detect	To TS816
15	Transmit clock	To TS816
17	Receive clock	To TS816
20	Data terminal ready	From TS816
24	Transmit clock	From TS816

Company: Texas Instruments, Inc.
Product: Business System 200
Port: EIA   Pin Configuration: C01

Pin	Function	Direction
1	Protective ground	N/A
2	Transmitted data	From 200
3	Received data	To 200
4	Request to send	From 200
5	Clear to send	To 200
6	Data set ready	To 200
7	Signal ground	N/A
8	Rec. line signal detector	To 200
11	Secondary request to send	From 200
12	Secondary RLSD	To 200
17	Receive signal timing	To 200
19	Secondary request to send	From 200
20	Data terminal ready	From 200
22	Ring indicator	To 200
24	Transmit signal timing	From 200

Note: Pins 17 and 24 are not used on asynchronous ports. A COMM option allows two more ports to be present—one asynchronous and one synchronous.

Company: Texas Instruments, Inc.
Product: 810 Printer
Port: Serial   Pin Configuration: P07

Pin	Function	Direction
1	Chassis ground	N/A
2	Transmitted data	From printer
3	Received data	To printer
6	Data set ready	To printer
7	Signal ground	N/A
8	Carrier detect	To printer
11	Reverse channel	From printer
20	Data terminal ready	From printer

Notes: (a) Pins 6 and 8 must be on for the printer to receive data. (b) Pin 11 can be used for flow control on the standard printer, whereas pin 20 is used on the DNB version for flow control.

Company: Texas Instruments, Inc.
Product: 820/840 Printers
Port: EIA   Pin Configuration: P05

Pin	Function	Direction
1	Protective ground	N/A
2	Transmitted data	From printer
3	Received data	To printer
4	Request to send	From printer
5	Clear to send	To printer
6	Data set ready	To printer
7	Signal ground	N/A
8	Rec. line signal detector	To printer
11	Ready/busy	From printer
12	Secondary RLSD	To printer
20	Data terminal ready	From printer
22	Ring indicator	To printer
23	Data signal rate selector	From printer

Notes: (a) Pin 22 is not used on the 840 printer. (b) Pins 5 and 6 must be on for transmission to occur. (c) Pins 6 and 8 must be on for reception to occur. (d) Pin 23 is held on to indicate 1200 bps speed on a dual-speed modem. (e) Pin 11 is used for flow control.

Company: Texas Instruments, Inc.
Product: TI940 Terminal
Port: COMM   Pin Configuration: T01

Pin	Function	Direction
1	Protective ground	N/A
2	Transmitted data	From 940
3	Received data	To 940
4	Request to send	From 940
5	Clear to send	To 940
6	Data set ready	To 940
7	Signal ground	N/A
8	Rec. line signal detector	To 940
11	Reverse channel transmit	From 940
12	Secondary RLSD	To 940
15	Transmit signal timing	To 940
17	Recive signal timing	To 940
19	Secondary request to send	From 940
20	Data terminal ready	From 940
21	Signal quality detector	To 940
22	Ring indicator	To 940
23	Data signal rate selector	From 940
24	Transmit signal timing	From 940

Notes: (a) The 940 will not transmit data unless pin 6 is on. (b) The 940 will not receive data unless pins 6 and 8 are on. (c) Pin 11 may be used for ready/busy indicator.

Company: Texas Instruments, Inc.
Product: 99/4 Computer
Port: RS-232   Pin Configuration: C02

Pin	Function	Direction
2	Serial data in	To 99/4
3	Serial data out	From 99/4
5	Clear to send	From 99/4
6	Data set ready	From 99/4
7	Signal ground	N/A
8	Data carrier detect	From 99/4
20	Data terminal ready	To 99/4

Company: Texas Instruments, Inc.
Product: Insight Series 10
Port: EIA   Pin Configuration: T01

Pin	Function	Direction
1	Protective ground	N/A
2	Transmitted data	From Series 10
3	Received data	To Series 10
4	Request to send	From Series 10
6	Data set ready	To Series 10
7	Signal ground	N/A
8	Rec. line signal detector	To Series 10
12	Secondary RLSD (EIA busy)	To Series 10
20	Data terminal ready	From Series 10

Note: Pin 12 can be used for busy status indicator.

Company: Texas Instruments, Inc.
Product: 820 RO
Port: EIA   Pin Configuration: P05

Pin	Function	Direction
1	Protective ground	N/A
2	Transmitted data	From 820
3	Received data	To 820
4	Request to send	From 820
5	Clear to send	To 820
6	Data set ready	To 820
7	Signal ground	N/A
8	Rec. line signal detector	To 820
11	Secondary request to send	From 820
12	Secondary RLSD	To 820
20	Data terminal ready	From 820
23	Data signal rate selector	From 820

Notes: (a) Pins 5, 6, and 8 must be on for the 820 to transmit data. (b) Pin 6 must be on for the 820 to receive data. (c) Pin 23 is used by the 820 to select data rates when used with dual-speed modems. (d) Pin 11 is used for printer busy status.

Company: Texas Instruments, Inc.
Product: Silent 745 Printer
Port: EIA   Pin Configuration: P01

Pin	Function	Direction
1	Protective ground	N/A
2	Transmitted data	From printer
3	Received data	To printer
4	Request to send	From printer
7	Signal ground	N/A
8	Data carrier detect	To printer
20	Data terminal ready	From printer

Note: Because this printer supports only 110/300-bps operation and prints at 10/30 cps, no flow control is required.

Company: Texas Instruments, Inc.
Product: Silent 781/783/785/787 Printers
Port: EIA   Pin Configuration: P05

Pin	Function	Direction
1	Protective ground	N/A
2	Transmitted data	From printer
3	Received data	To printer
4	Request to send	From printer
5	Clear to send	To printer
6	Data set ready	To printer
7	Signal ground	N/A
8	Rec. line signal detector	To printer
11	Secondary request to send	From printer
12	Secondary RLSD	To printer
20	Data terminal ready	From printer
22	Ring indicator	To printer
23	Data signal rate selector	From printer

Notes: (a) XON/XOFF is supported by the printers. (b) Pin 11 may be used for hardware flow control.

Company: Toshiba America Inc.
Product: T100/200/250 Computers
Port: Serial   Pin Configuration: C01

Pin	Function	Direction
1	Protective ground	N/A
2	Transmitted data	From computer
3	Received data	To computer
4	Request to send	From computer
5	Clear to send	To computer
6	Data set ready	To computer
7	Signal ground	N/A
20	Data terminal ready	From computer

Company: Toshiba America Inc.
Product: P1350 Printer
Port: Serial   Pin Configuration: P08

Pin	Function	Direction
1	Protective ground	N/A
2	Transmitted data	From P1350
3	Received data	To P1350
7	Signal ground	N/A
20	Data terminal ready	From P1350

Note: Pin 20 is used for flow control.

Company: Vector Graphic, Inc.
Product: Vector 4 Computer
Port: Serial   Pin Configuration: C01

Pin	Function	Direction
2	Transmitted data	From Vector 4
3	Received data	To Vector 4
4	Clear to send	To Vector 4
5	Clear to send	From Vector 4
6	Data set ready	To Vector 4
7	Ground	N/A
20	Data terminal ready	From Vector 4

Company: Vector Graphic, Inc.
Product: Vector 4 Computer
Port: Modem   Pin Configuration: C01

Pin	Function	Direction
2	Transmitted data	From Vector 4
3	Received data	To Vector 4
4	Request to send	From Vector 4
5	Clear to send	To Vector 4
6	Data set ready	To Vector 4
7	Ground	N/A
20	Data terminal ready	From Vector 4

Company: Vector Graphic, Inc.
Product: Bitstreamer II Board
Port: A, B, and C   Pin Configuration: C09

Pin	Function	Direction
1	Protective ground	N/A
2	Transmitted data	To Bitstreamer
3	Received data	From Bitstreamer
4	Request to send	To Bitstreamer
5	Clear to send	From Bitstreamer
6	Data set ready	From Bitstreamer
7	Signal ground	N/A
8	Rec. line signal detector	From Bitstreamer
12	Secondary RLSD	From Bitstreamer
13	Secondary clear to send	From Bitstreamer
14	Secondary transmitted data	To Bitstreamer
16	Secondary received data	From Bitstreamer
19	Secondary request to send	To Bitstreamer
20	Data terminal ready	To Bitstreamer

Notes: (a) Synchronous operation of these ports is supported. (b) This board is used on the 5000 series computers.

Company: Vector Graphic, Inc.
Product: ZCB Board
Port: Serial   Pin Configuration: C09

Pin	Function	Direction
1	Protective ground	N/A
2	Received data	To ZCB
3	Transmitted data	From ZCB
4	Clear to send	To ZCB
5	Request to send	From ZCB
6	Data terminal ready	From ZCB
20	Data set ready	To ZCB

Note: This board is used in the 2600 and 3000 series computers.

Company: Victor Business Products
Product: 9000 Computer
Port: TTY and UL1   Pin Configuration: C01

Pin	Function	Direction
1	Chassis ground	N/A
2	Transmitted data	From 9000
3	Received data	To 9000
4	Request to send	From 9000
5	Clear to send	To 9000
6	Data set ready	To 9000
7	Signal ground	N/A
8	Data carrier detect	To 9000
15	Transmit clock	To 9000
17	Receive clock	To 9000
20	Data terminal ready	From 9000
22	Ring indicator	To 9000

Company: Xerox Corporation
Product: 820/820-2 Computer
Port: Communication (J4)   Pin Configuration: C01

Pin	Function	Direction
1	Protective ground	N/A
2	Transmitted data	From 820
3	Received data	To 820
4	Request to send	From 820
5	Clear to send	To 820
6	Data set ready	To 820
7	Signal ground	N/A
8	Data carrier detect	To 820
20	Data terminal ready	From 820

Note: Pin 6 is always on.

Company: Xerox Corporation
Product: 820/820-2 Computer
Port: Printer (J3)   Pin Configuration: C14

Pin	Function	Direction
1	Protective ground	N/A
2	Data in	To 820
3	Data out	From 820
4	Request to send	To 820
5	Clear to send	From 820
6	Data set ready	From 820
7	Signal ground	N/A
8	Data carrier detect	From 820
20	Data terminal ready	To 820

Notes: (a) A printer interface kit is available for the 820, giving it an XON/XOFF capability, and pin 20 can then be monitored for hardware flow control. Without this kit, ETX/ACK is available. (b) With the 820-2, XON/XOFF is standard. Also, under the CP/M operating system, pin 20 or pin 4 may be monitored for flow control.

Company: Xerox Corporation
Product: 1700 Printer
Port: Serial   Pin Configuration: P10

Pin	Function	Direction
1	Protective ground	N/A
2	Transmitted data	From 1700
3	Received data	To 1700
4	Request to send	From 1700
5	Clear to send	To 1700
6	Data set ready	To 1700
7	Signal ground	N/A
8	Data carrier detect	To 1700
20	Data terminal ready	From 1700

Notes: (a) Pin 5 must be on to enable the 1700 to transmit. (b) Pin 6 must be on to enable the 1700 to receive. (c) Uses XON/XOFF for flow control.

Company: Xerox Corporation
Product: 1730 Printer
Port: Serial   Pin Configuration: P05

Pin	Function	Direction
1	Protective ground	N/A
2	Transmitted data	From 1730
3	Received data	To 1730
4	Request to send	From 1730
5	Clear to send	To 1730
6	Data set ready	To 1730
7	Signal ground	N/A
8	Rec. line signal detector	To 1730
11	Printer ready	From 1730
20	Data terminal ready	From 1730

Notes: (a) Pin 20 can be optioned for printer ready function. (b) Pin 6 must be on to receive data.

Company: Xerox Corporation
Product: 1740/1750 Printers
Port: Serial   Pin Configuration: P03

Pin	Function	Direction
1	Protective ground	N/A
2	Transmitted data	From printer
3	Received data	To printer
4	Request to send	From printer
5	Clear to send	To printer
6	Data set ready	To printer
7	Signal ground	N/A
8	Data carrier detect	To printer
20	Data terminal ready	From printer

Notes: (a) Pin 6 must be on to receive data. (b) Pin 5 must be on to send data. (c) Pin 20 can provide printer ready signal.

Company: Zenith Data Systems, Inc.
Product: Z-25 Printer
Port: Serial   Pin Configuration: P12

Pin	Function	Direction
1	Protective ground	N/A
2	Serial output	From Z-25
3	Serial input	To Z-25
4	Busy	From Z-25
7	Signal common	N/A

Notes: (a) Pin 4 should be used for flow control. (b) The cable supplied with the printer provides pins 1–7, 11, and 20 straight through.

Company: Zenith Data Systems, Inc.
Product: Z-89 Computer
Port: DTE   Pin Configuration: C01

Pin	Function	Direction
1	Protective ground	N/A
2	Transmitted data	From Z-89
3	Received data	To Z-89
4	Request to send	From Z-89
5	Clear to send	To Z-89
6	Data set ready	To Z-89
7	Signal ground	N/A
8	Rec. line signal detector	To Z-89
20	Data terminal ready	From Z-89

Note: The DTE port is designated as 330/337.

Company: Zenith Data Systems, Inc.
Product: Z-89 Computer
Port: Printer and DCE   Pin Configuration: C09

Pin	Function	Direction
1	Protective ground	N/A
2	Transmitted data	To Z-89
3	Received data	From Z-89
4	Request to send	To Z-89
5	Clear to send	From Z-89
6	Data set ready	From Z-89
7	Signal ground	N/A
8	Rec. line signal detector	From Z-89
20	Data terminal ready	To Z-89

Note: The printer and DCE ports are designated as 340/347 and 320/327, respectively.

Company: Zilog
Product: System 8000, Models 10, 11, 21, and 31
Port: TTY   Pin Configuration: C09

Pin	Function	Direction
2	Transmitted data	To 8000
3	Received data	From 8000
4	Request to send	To 8000
5	Clear to send	From 8000
6	Data set ready	From 8000
7	Signal ground	N/A
20	Data terminal ready	To 8000

Notes: (a) There is no hardware flow control, but the system does support XON/XOFF characters. (b) Pin 20 can be used to control the system status; however, it is not generally considered to perform flow control.

G

Interconnections Between Computers and Peripherals

Appendix G outlines the connections of computers, terminals, and printers through an RS-232 port. When used in conjunction with Appendix F, the proper cables may be constructed to allow data exchange between devices.

The following displays the step-by-step procedure for determining how the pins of RS-232 cables should be connected.

1. In Appendix F, locate the appropriate devices to be connected, noting their corresponding pin configuration. (If your device is not listed, compare its RS-232 pin assignments with devices in Appendix F until a match is found. Then, use that pin configuration as a surrogate.)
2. Proceed to the appropriate table in this appendix. Figure G-1 is for connecting computers to printers; while Figure G-2 is for connecting computers to terminals (CRTs).

	Printer														
Computer	P01	P02	P03	P04	P05	P06	P07	P08	P09	P10	P11	P12	P13	P14	P15
C01	G01	G02	G03	G04	G04	G05	G06	G05	G07	G08	G05	G07	G01	G09	G10
C02	G11	G12	G12	G13	G13	G12	G13	G12	G14	G12	G12	G14	G11	G15	G16
C03	G13	G12	G17	G13	G13	G17	G13	G17	G12	G12	G17	G12	G13	G15	G16
C04	G19	G18	G20	G21	G21	G20	G21	G20	G18	G18	G22	G18	G19	G09	G10
C05	G19	G18	G20	G21	G21	G20	G21	G20	G18	G18	G22	G18	G19	G09	G10
C06	G23	G12	G23	G23	G23	G12	G23	G12	G23	G23	G23	G24	G23	G38	G23
C07	G26	G18	G27	G21	G21	G22	G21	G22	G07	G25	G08	G18	G01	G09	G10
C08	G01	G07	G08	G04	G04	G03	G06	G22	G07	G22	G08	G18	G19	G09	G10
C09	G12	G28	G29	G12	G12	G29	G12	G29	G28	G12	G29	G28	G12	G15	G29
C10	G30	G30	G30	G30	G30	G12	G12	G12	G30	G30	G12	G30	G30	G15	G30
C11	G01	G18	G03	G04	G04	G05	G06	G05	G07	G08	G05	G07	G01	G09	G10
C12	G24	G24	G31	G32	G32	G12	G32	G12	G33	G31	G12	G33	G24	G09	G34
C13	G24	G24	G31	G32	G32	G31	G35	G31	G33	G34	G31	G33	G24	G15	G36
C14	G24	G34	G12	G37	G37	G12	G37	G12	G14	G30	G12	G14	G11	G38	G34
C15	G24	G24	G31	G32	G32	G31	G35	G31	G33	G31	G39	G33	G24	G40	G41

Figure G–1

Terminal (CRT)		
Computer	T01	T04
C01	G01	G03
C02	G11	G12
C03	G12	G17
C04	G19	G20
C05	G19	G20
C06	G23	G23
C07	G26	G27
C08	G01	G08
C09	G12	G29
C10	G30	G30
C11	G01	G03
C12	G24	G31
C13	G24	G31
C14	G24	G12
C15	G24	G31

Figure G–2

3. Find the pin configuration for the computer in the column labeled "Computer" at the left of the table.
4. Find the proper pin configuration for the printer or terminal across the top of the table.
5. Note the diagram number at the intersection of the row and column.
6. Find the appropriately labeled graph in this appendix for a display of the cross connections necessary in the RS-232 cable. Construct the cable accordingly. For example, to connect computer C01 to printer P10, use diagram G08.

It is important to note that when building RS-232 cables, many different combinations of pin configurations exist for a connection. The diagrams point out only one of many ways in which RS-232 leads may be connected. Neither the author nor the publisher claims responsibility for the accuracy of the diagrams or charts, as they were constructed from information supplied by the vendors. The vendors of these products often provide similar information for device connections. Use their recommendations when possible, as they have been thoroughly tested. This should be done also because, in some cases, more leads are present in the diagrams than are actually needed. They are provided for completeness.

For example, often pin 19, 20, or 4 may be used to hold a given lead, such as data set ready, on or off. The choice may be dictated by a factor such as flow control. If hardware flow control will not be used, pin 4 or 20 would be selected, in which case pin 19 would not even be used. The selection should be based on the options for the particular installation.

Furthermore, different configurations may be possible for ports. The way a port is configured affects the cable to be used. If a port may be set up to emulate either data communications equipment or data terminal equipment, choose the configuration that allows for the most flexibility in your configuration.

Once the cable has been built, the options should be reviewed as described in Chapter 8. They are as follows:

Speed	Flow control
Parity	Character length
Number of stop bits	Mode
Echoplex	Line feeds
Transmission control	Polarity

Double-check to ensure that these are properly set. Once set, attach the cable between the devices, power up the devices, enable the ports, and test your system for proper operation.

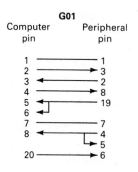

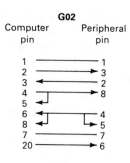

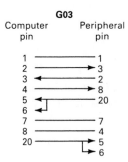

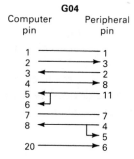

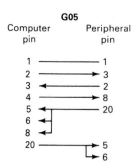

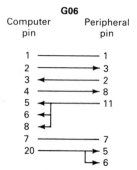

G07

Computer pin		Peripheral pin
1	———————	1
2	———————►	3
3	◄———————	2
4	———————►	8
5	◄———	4
6	◄———	5
8	◄———	
7	———————	7
20	———————►	6

G08

Computer pin		Peripheral pin
1	———————	1
2	———————►	3
3	◄———————	2
4	———————►	8
5	◄———	20
6	◄———	
7	———————	7
8	◄———————	4
20	———————►	5
	►	6

G09

Computer pin		Peripheral pin
1	———————	1
2	———————	2
5	◄———	8
6	◄———	
8	◄———	
20	◄———	
7	———————	7

G10

Computer pin		Peripheral pin
1	———————	1
2	———————►	3
3	◄———————	2
4	———————►	8
5	◄———	25
6	◄———	
7	———————	7
8	◄———————	4
	►	5
	►	6

G11

Computer pin		Peripheral pin
1	———————	1
2	———————	2
3	———————	3
4	———————	4
5	———————	5
6	———————	6
7	———————	7
8	———————	8
		11
20	◄———	19
12	———————	12

G12

Computer pin		Peripheral pin
1	———————	1
2	———————	2
3	———————	3
4	———————	4
5	———————	5
6	———————	6
7	———————	7
8	———————	8
11	———————	11
12	———————	12
19	———————	19
20	———————	20
22	———————	22

G13

Computer pin	Peripheral pin
1 ——————— 1	
2 ——————— 2	
3 ——————— 3	
4 ◄———— 11	
20 ◄———— 19	
5 ——————— 5	
6 ——————— 6	
7 ——————— 7	
8 ——————— 8	

G14

Computer pin	Peripheral pin
1 ——————— 1	
2 ——————— 2	
3 ——————— 3	
4 ◄———— 4	
20 ◄	
5 ————► 5	
►► 6	
7 ——————— 7	
8 ——————— 8	

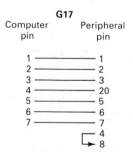

G15

Computer pin	Peripheral pin
1 ——————— 1	
3 ◄———— 2	
4 ———— 8	
5 ◄	
19 ◄	
20 ◄	
7 ——————— 7	

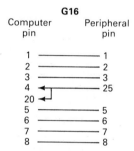

G16

Computer pin	Peripheral pin
1 ——————— 1	
2 ——————— 2	
3 ——————— 3	
4 ◄———— 25	
20 ◄	
5 ——————— 5	
6 ——————— 6	
7 ——————— 7	
8 ——————— 8	

G17

Computer pin	Peripheral pin
1 ——————— 1	
2 ——————— 2	
3 ——————— 3	
4 ——————— 20	
5 ——————— 5	
6 ——————— 6	
7 ——————— 7	
►► 4	
8	

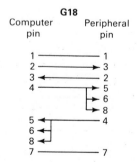

G18

Computer pin	Peripheral pin
1 ——————— 1	
2 ————► 3	
3 ◄———— 2	
4 ————► 5	
►► 6	
►► 8	
5 ◄———— 4	
6 ◄	
8 ◄	
7 ——————— 7	

G19

Computer pin   Peripheral pin

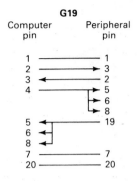

G20

Computer pin   Peripheral pin

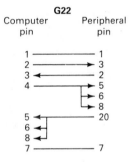

G21

Computer pin   Peripheral pin

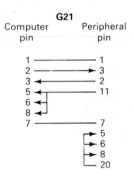

G22

Computer pin   Peripheral pin

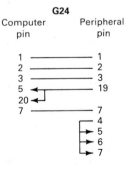

G23

Computer pin   Peripheral pin

G24

Computer pin   Peripheral pin

G25

Computer pin   Peripheral pin

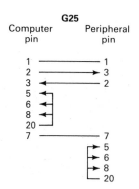

```
1 ———————— 1
2 ————————▶ 3
3 ◀———————— 2
5 ◀┐
6 ◀┤
8 ◀┤
20 ┘
7 ———————— 7
        ┌▶ 5
        ├▶ 6
        ├▶ 8
        └ 20
```

G26

Computer pin   Peripheral pin

```
1 ———————— 1
2 ———————— 3
3 ———————— 2
5 ◀———————— 19
6 ◀┐
8 ◀┤
7 ———————— 7
20 ————————▶ 5
         ┌▶ 6
         └▶ 8
```

G27

Computer pin   Peripheral pin

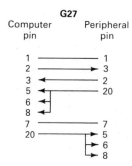

```
1 ———————— 1
2 ————————▶ 3
3 ◀———————— 2
5 ◀┐ ———————— 20
6 ◀┤
8 ◀┤
7 ———————— 7
20 ————————▶ 5
         ┌▶ 6
         └▶ 8
```

G28

Computer pin   Peripheral pin

```
1 ———————— 1
2 ———————— 2
3 ———————— 3
4 ———————— 4
11 ◀┐
19 ◀┤
20 ◀┘
5 ———————— 5
6 ———————— 6
7 ———————— 7
8 ———————— 8
```

G29

Computer pin   Peripheral pin

```
1 ———————— 1
2 ———————— 2
3 ———————— 3
4 ———————— 4
5 ———————— 5
6 ———————— 6
7 ———————— 7
8 ———————— 8
19 ◀┐ ———————— 20
20 ◀┘
```

G30

Computer pin   Peripheral pin

```
1 ———————— 1
2 ———————— 2
3 ———————— 3
          ┌ 4
          ├▶ 5
          └▶ 6
7 ———————— 7
8 ———————— 8
20 ———————— 20
```

G31

Computer pin		Peripheral pin
1	———————	1
2	———————	2
3	———————	3
		4
		5
		6
		8
7	———————	7
5		20
6		
20		

G32

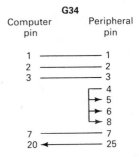

Computer pin		Peripheral pin
1	———————	1
2	———————	2
3	———————	3
		4
		5
		6
		8
5		11
20		
7	———————	7

G33

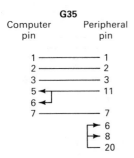

Computer pin		Peripheral pin
1	———————	1
2	———————	2
3	———————	3
		4
5		5
20		6
7	———————	7

G34

Computer pin		Peripheral pin
1	———————	1
2	———————	2
3	———————	3
		4
		5
		6
		8
7	———————	7
20		25

G35

Computer pin		Peripheral pin
1	———————	1
2	———————	2
3	———————	3
5		11
6		
7	———————	7
		6
		8
		20

G36

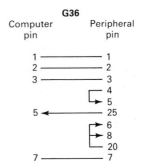

Computer pin		Peripheral pin
1	———————	1
2	———————	2
3	———————	3
		4
		5
5		25
		6
		8
		20
7	———————	7

G37

Computer pin		Peripheral pin
1	————————	1
2	————————	2
3	————————	3
4	————————	4
5	————————	5
		6
8	————————	8
7	————————	7
20	◄————————	11

G38

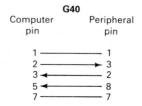

Computer pin		Peripheral pin
1	————————	1
2	————————►	3
3	◄————————	2
4	————————	4
5	————————	5
7	————————	7
20	◄————————	8

G39

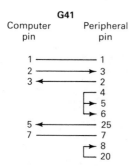

Computer pin		Peripheral pin
1	————————	1
2	————————	2
3	————————	3
5	◄	► 6
6	◄	20
7	————————	7

G40

Computer pin		Peripheral pin
1	————————	1
2	————————►	3
3	◄————————	2
5	◄————————	8
7	————————	7

G41

Computer pin		Peripheral pin
1	————————	1
2	————————►	3
3	◄————————	2
		4
	►	5
		6
5	◄————————	25
7	————————	7
		8
		20

G42

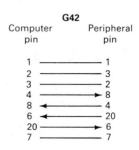

Computer pin		Peripheral pin
1	————————	1
2	————————	3
3	————————	2
4	————————►	8
8	◄————————	4
6	◄————————	20
20	————————►	6
7	————————	7

H

Interfacing Problems and Remedies

Symptom	Equipment	Cause/Remedy
Improper spacing Double spacing	Terminal or printer	Line feeds; see if computer outputs a line feed with each carriage return. If so, option for "0" line feeds at the device, or option the computer to only output a carriage return. If not, device should be optioned for single spacing.
No spacing	Terminal or printer	Computer is only outputting a carriage return, while the device is not adding a line feed. Option either the computer or the device to add a line feed with each carriage return.
No data is being displayed or printed	Terminal or printer	Check to be sure power is on. Ensure that device is in on-line mode. RS-232 port requirements may not be satisfied. Check manuals or Appendixes F and G for cabling assistance. Polarity of signals could be improperly set. Both ends should be set the same. Speed of the ports may not be set the same. Device controller may be defective; run self test according to the user manuals. Cables may not be plugged snuggly into port.
	Printer	Possibly out of paper. Printer lid, if raised, may inhibit further printing. Computer or terminal port to which printer is attached may be incorrectly configured as DCE or DTE; verify this. Printer ribbon may be defective or worn out; replace. Computer port driving the printer may not be enabled.
Garbled or lost data	Terminal, printer, or computer	Port speeds may not be consistent. Cable could be faulty. Character lengths could be wrong. Flow control may not be occurring. Parity may be improperly set.
Communication line cannot be established or maintained	Terminal, printer, or computer	Power may be off on the device. This would disable pin 20, Data Terminal Ready, which should not allow the connection to be made. Ensure that the device is powered on. Device or port must be in on-line mode to keep DTR on and maintain the line. Duplex should be the same at each end. Computer at the far end may automatically disconnect if it determines that the call is being made by an invalid user. Cable between the device and the modem may be faulty or not properly wired.
	Modem	Power must be on. Modem cannot be in test mode. Modem is defective; run self test. Modem must be compatible with the modem at the other end. For example, the modulation techniques must be compatible. Duplex must be consistent at both ends.

Bibliography

BELL SYSTEM TECHNICAL REFERENCE, Pub. 41106, 103J Data Set.

BELL SYSTEM TECHNICAL REFERENCE, Pub. 41214, 212A Data Set.

BELL SYSTEM TECHNICAL REFERENCE, Pub. 41212, 202S and 202T Data Set.

ELECTRONIC INDUSTRIES ASSOCIATION, EIA Standard RS-232-C, Washington, D.C.: 1969.

MARTIN, JAMES. *Telecommunications and the Computer*. Englewood Cliffs, N.J.: Prentice-Hall, Inc., 1976.

MCNAMARA, JOHN E. *Technical Aspects of Data Communications*. Bedford, Mass. Digital Press, 1978.

Index